Table of Contents

Outlaws

and

Gunslingers

By Alton Pryor

Stagecoach Publishing
Roseville, California

Outlaws and Gunslingers

ISBN: 0-9660053-6-8
First Edition

First Printing 2001

Stagecoach Publishing

5360 Campcreek Loop
Roseville, CA. 95747
Phone: (916) 771-8166
Email: pryor@jps.net

Outlaws

and

Gunslingers

Tales of the West's Most Notorious Outlaws

Other Books by Alton Pryor

"Little Known Tales in California History"
ISBN: 0-9660053-1-7: $9.95

"Classic Tales in California History"
ISBN: 0-9660053-2-5: $9.95

"Jonathan's Red Apple Tree"
ISBN: 0-9660053-3-3: $6.95

"Those Wild and Lusty Gold Camps"
ISBN: 0-9660053-4-1: $6.95

Chapter 1

Billy the Kid

It's hard to imagine that so much activity could have been crammed into any one man's life as short as that of Billy the Kid. Billy was born on November 23, 1859 and died July 14, 1881.

"Did Billy the Kid intentionally become an outlaw, or was he driven to it?" There are so many inconsistencies in the hundreds of Billy the Kid reports that the question remains perplexing.

Just pinpointing where Billy the Kid was born has been a difficult task for historians. Some say he was born in New York City, some say in Indiana, and still others put his birth in Missouri.

The most plausible seems to be that he was born in an Irish section of New York City's disease-infested slums in 1859, the son of Catherine and William McCarty. They named their son William Henry McCarty.

When his father died, Billy's mother later married William Antrim. Billy and his brother Joe were witnesses at that wedding. The family eventually traveled west to Silver City, New Mexico, where Billy's mother operated a boarding house. His mother died Sept. 16, 1874 after a short illness, apparently from tuberculosis.

It was in Silver City that Billy first ran counter to the law. He was about 15 years old when he and a companion, George "Sombrero Jack" Shaffer, were arrested for stealing clothes from a Chinese laundry.

While the theft was said to be an adolescent prank, Billy was jailed. He escaped from the jail by squeezing his wiry frame through the chimney of the jail. He then decided to leave home rather than face the anger of his stern stepfather.

The accounts that claim Billy the Kid had killed 21 men during his 21-year life span are generally considered myths that have built up into a legend that is difficult to either document or disprove. It is known that he killed at least four men.

Billy the Kid

One undocumented account says Billy killed his first man in Coffeyville, Kansas, even before he and his family had left that town for New Mexico. Billy was said to have also killed three Apache braves near the Chiracachua Reservation a few years later. None were ever proved.

He is blamed for killing a blacksmith in Fort Bowie, three cardsharks in Mexico, and two more Indians in the Guadalupe Mountains, among others along the way. These were never proved either.

It is known that he had an argument with an Irish blacksmith, named Frank Cahill, in Camp Grant, Arizona on August 17, 1877. Billy, then 17-years-old, was in a saloon when the event happened. The bullying blacksmith called Billy a pimp, slapped his face, and threw him on the floor, pinning the youngster's arms down with his knees while continuing to beat on him.

Billy begged the blacksmith to stop, as he was hurting him. The blacksmith roared that he wanted to hurt him.

Billy knew he was no match for the burly man. He managed to get one hand on his Colt .45, drew it and fired. The blacksmith died the following day. Billy was locked up in the post guardhouse, but he easily escaped and began running.

It is believed about this time he adopted the alias of William H. Bonney. After the fracas with the blacksmith, Billy drifted among cow camps on the New Mexico-Arizona border. Sometimes, he made short stops in small towns and mining camps to gamble, drink, and work at odd jobs to earn a little money.

Billy the Kid's Gun

He eventually ended up in Lincoln County, New Mexico. During his drifting, Billy stopped at the Coe Ranch, where he met George Coe and his cousin Frank. It was through the Coes that Billy first learned of the hate and bitterness growing in Lincoln County. The matter soon burgeoned into a full-blown battle.

On one side of the issue was John Chisum, the cattle king of Lincoln County, John Henry Tunstall, and Alexander McSween, an attorney. Chisum's spread was the largest ranch in the West, with more than 60,000 head of cattle grazing the open land.

On the other side, was L.G. Murphy & Co. Lawrence Murphy owned a huge general store called "The House". Murphy pretty much controlled the law in the town along with everything else.

He eventually sold "The House" to J.J. Dolan and John Riley, who then controlled the power in the county. A big issue was who would control government contracts to supply beef to Army posts and Indian reservations?

Tunstall did not feel one outfit should control so much power as the owners of "The House." He bought a sizeable ranch in the county, but also defiantly challenged Dolan and Riley's big general store by building a competing store in Lincoln.

He made his prices competitive and won many of the rancher accounts over from Dolan and Riley, which infuriated the powerful pair. Dolan and Riley issued immediate threats of arson and even death if Tunstall didn't desist.

Consequently, Tunstall, Chisum and McSween were forced to hire bodyguards for protection. It was into this fray that walked Billy the Kid.

In 1877, Billy the Kid, a gun-proud youngster, entered the services of John Tunstall. Billy worshiped Tunstall. He said, "He was the only man who ever treated me kindly, like I was free born and white."

Billy proved loyal and showed Tunstall he also had savvy. While his small wiry frame and boyish smile did not fit the standard of a bodyguard, his lightning quick draw and willingness to challenge enemies made up for it.

"That's the finest lad I ever met," Tunstall told his partner Chisum. "He's a revelation to me every day and would do anything to please me. He has his immature ways, but bless me, I'm going to make a man out of that boy some day. You wait and see."

Chisum's ranch hands were hired not only for their ability to handle cattle, but also for their adeptness with guns. They were charged with driving away homesteaders or other small ranchers that wanted to settle in the area.

Riley and Dolan then trumped up charges against Tunstall, claiming he had stolen some cattle. A paid-off judge, who heard the charges, upheld them. When Sheriff William Brady and his posse attempted to confiscate part of his cattle herd to pay what Tunstall considered an illegal judgment, Tunstall was killed.

Tunstall's murder was a real turning point in Billy's life. He flipped crazily with anger. Billy became deeply embroiled in what is known as "The Lincoln County War". This involvement initiated Billy into the real world of outlawry.

At that time, Lincoln County covered nearly one-fifth of the entire New Mexico territory. It was the largest county in the United States.

The killing of Tunstall roused not only Billy but also his other ranch hands, which soon formed a group called the "Regulators". They vowed to run down the killers and avenge the murder of the Tunstall.

Billy the Kid was a strong member of the Regulators. He and other cowhands working for Tunstall had witnessed Jesse Evans shoot Tunstall through the chest. They had also witnessed Deputy Billy Morton smash Tunstall's skull with the butt of his rifle after the man had been shot.

Four days later, the Regulators, with Billy among them, captured Frank Baker and Billy Morton. Both men were shot execution-style and left for the buzzards to devour.

The Regulators continued hunting Tunstall's killers, including Sheriff William Brady who was in charge of the posse that killed Tunstall. While Brady and two of his deputies were walking down the street in Lincoln, the

Regulators opened fire on them from behind an adobe wall.

There is little if any evidence to show exactly who the triggerman was in the shooting, but the blame was laid on Billy the Kid. Here the "Kid's" reputation began its legendary spiral upward.

With the killing of Sheriff Brady, murder warrants were issued. It was the killing of Sheriff Brady and his deputies that launched the young outlaw's reputation as one of the most feared gunmen in the west.

It became clear that anyone having associated with the Tunstall, McSween, and Chisum forces was no longer safe in Lincoln County and vigilante committees were forming to deal with them.

Eventually, Billy was captured and taken to Mesilla, New Mexico, where he was convicted of the killings of Sheriff Brady and his two deputies. While in jail, Billy seized a chance to escape while prison guard Bob Ollinger took other prisoners across the street to eat.

Billy, left in solitary, summoned his guard, J.W. Bell, and asked to be taken to the outhouse. On the way back up the stairs, Billy slipped his very small hands from the handcuffs.

While hobbling in leg chains, he knocked Bell down and made it into a gunroom a few feet away. There he grabbed a pistol, and as Bell came running into the room, ordering him to put the pistol down. Billy replied, "Sorry, Bell," and shot the deputy dead.

One report says Billy then hobbled to the outside second-story balcony, armed with a shotgun to await the return of Deputy Bob Ollinger, whom he hated.

"Hello, Bob," Billy called out. As Ollinger looked up to see Billy on the balcony, the outlaw let loose both barrels of the shotgun, blasting Ollinger several feet into the ruts of the road.

When Billy read in a newspaper that Jim Dolan, one of the owners of "The House", was in custody for the back shooting of Huston Chapman, a Regulator, The Kid conceived a somewhat brilliant plan.

He had witnessed Dolan's crime and decided to turn state's evidence in return for his own life. According to writer Jay Robert Nash, author of Western Lawmen and Outlaws, Billy, on March 17, 1879, rapped the huge metallic knocker on the door of the Governor's Mansion in Santa Fe.

When a clerk answered the door, Billy said, "I'd like to see the man who wants to hang me. This is Billy the Kid." After surrendering his Remington and Colt firearms, Billy was taken to Governor Lee Wallace.

According to author Nash, Wallace at first couldn't believe it, thinking someone was pulling a joke on him. Could this young boy be the most-wanted outlaw in the West?

Wallace asked, "Are you surrendering yourself, Kid?"

"Maybe, on condition," the Kid replied. "Only on condition."

Billy admitted he had killed Brady and Hindman, but only after they had shot Tunstall in cold blood.

"In other words," said Governor Wallace, "you want to turn state's witness for your life."

"It sounds kind of harsh that way, but I guess that's it," replied Billy. "But you'll get no testimony about my friends, only about my enemies."

Governor Wallace considered the proposition for a moment. "Billy," he said, "you're a lad of cunning mettle. You stroll in here and offer yourself up to the gods who you know want to toss you into the volcano as their sacrifice to themselves--and you dare to offer a compromise. I like a sharp man—and I'll take your wager."

Wallace agreed to have Billy arrested the next morning in a public house in Santa Fe.

Billy learned from the deputy guarding him that even after Jim Dolan was tried, Billy too would face a jury for killing Sheriff Brady.

This, Billy cursed, was not part of the deal he had made with Governor Wallace. He over-powered the deputy and again escaped from the law.

Billy the Kid was living in a powder-keg situation. He organized a gang of iron-nerved horse-thieves that included Tom O'Folliard, Dave Rudabaugh, Tom Pickett, and Billy Wilson.

This wily gang dedicated themselves to stealing horses all the way from central New Mexico to the Texas Panhandle and selling them to the highest bidder.

Finally, in desperation, New Mexico stockmen elected Patrick Garrett as sheriff of Lincoln County. His mission, "Capture Billy the Kid alive or dead!" Garrett spent three months tracking The Kid all over New Mexico.

Finally, on the night of July 14, 1881, Garrett rode onto the old Maxwell ranch where The Kid was visiting a Mexican woman. When he heard hoof beats, Billy stepped outside into the moonlight to see who the horsemen were.

Unknown to Billy, Garrett had entered the large ranch house, gone down a corridor and entered the darkened bedroom. Billy, from outside, called in a loud whisper, in Spanish: "Quien es? Quien es?" (Who is it?)

When no one answered, he stepped back through the outside door of the bedroom, only to see Garrett holding a gun on him. Garrett's first shot struck the outlaw in the heart, killing him instantly.

It took a special act of the territorial legislature before Garrett finally collected the $500 reward that was offered for the capture or killing of Billy the Kid.

There are varying accounts of Billy's true personality. The following accounts were taken from the WPA Files of the Library of Congress. A child friend of Billy was Berta Ballard. Billy frequently visited the Ballards and would hold Berta on his lap.

"He was kind and could be a good friend," she said, "but I am sure we should not make a hero of Billy, for after all he was a bandit and a killer."

Berta's brother, Charles L. Ballard, remembered the good times he had with Billy. "He was not an outlaw in manners. He was quiet, but good company, always doing something interesting. That was why he had so many friends. We often raced horses together. He was not very large – weighed a hundred and twenty five or thirty pounds. He was a fine rider."

In an interview with a reporter, Ballard said, "Billy was credited with more killings than he ever did. It was reported he was the one who killed Chapman, when Chapman refused to dance when ordered, but Billy had nothing at all to do with that shooting."

From the Library of Congress files is an interview with Amelia Bolton Church, who held a different view of Billy's murder of deputies Bell and Ollinger. Mrs. Church was a daughter of John Bolton, head of the Quartermaster Department at Fort Stanton, New Mexico.

"Up stairs in the old Court House at Lincoln is the room where Billy the Kid was confined waiting for trial for the killing of Major (Sheriff) Brady. There have been

19

many untrue stories told of the Kid's sensational escape after killing his two guards Bell and Ollinger. I remember all of the facts in connection with that escape."

Mrs. Church's interview continued: "Billy the Kid was playing cards with Deputy Jim Bell while Ollinger, the other guard, was at dinner across the street.

He saw his chance and grabbed Bell's gun. Bell darted down the inside stairway, but Billy the Kid was too quick for him, fired and Bell fell dead at the bottom of the stairs.

"Billy the Kid then walked calmly to a window and shot Ollinger down as he came running when he heard the shooting. The "Kid" then threw the gun on top of Ollinger who lay dying, and told Goss, the jail cook, to saddle a horse that was feeding in an alfalfa field nearby.

"The cook helped get the shackles off the Kid's hands, but because they were welded on he couldn't get them off his legs. That is why he was thrown from the horse because of having to ride sidewise on account of the shackles.

"He rode a mile and a half west before they were removed by a Mexican man, who afterwards gave the shackles to George Titsworth, who lived at Capitan, and possessed an interesting collection at that place."

Also from the WPA Files of the Library of Congress in an interview with Ella Bolton Davidson, who was the daughter of the postmaster in Lincoln, New Mexico.

She met Billy the Kid at a dancing party given by a woman hostess who shared the belief of many others that "The Kid" had been led into evil paths, and through kindness and friendliness of hospitality, might be led back into the "straight and narrow" way".

Mrs. Davidson told the interviewer, "Billy the Kid thoroughly enjoyed the party and the occasion of his dancing with Ella Bolton until in his exuberance of enjoyment of the dance, he lifted her and lightly swung her off her feet. Then he, who had boasted of conquests and murdering of numerous big strong men, was made ashamed when he was left on the dance floor, where he stood in confusion, vanquished by a small young girl."

From the WPA Library of Congress file on Francisco Gomez, telling of Billy's stay at the McSween ranch where he went to work at age 18, is the following:

"I remember that one winter Billy the Kid stayed with the McSweens for about seven months, I guess he boarded with them. He was an awfully nice young fellow with light brown hair, blue eyes, and rather big front teeth. He always dressed very neatly.

"He used to practice target shooting a lot. He would throw up a can and would twirl his six-gun on his finger and he could hit the can six times before it hit the ground. He rode a big roan horse about ten or twelve hands high. While the horse was out in the pasture, Billy would go to the gate and whistle and the horse would come up to the gate to him."

Obviously, Billy the Kid's outlaw escapades have grown feverously with every telling. When boiled down to known facts, historians can only account for four men killed by the feared desperado.

• Windy Frank Cahill: Billy killed Cahill on August 17, 1877 at Camp Grant Arizona. The killing came after the drunken blacksmith called Billy a pimp, threw him to the ground, and while holding Billy down with his knees, kept slapping the youth. Billy managed to pull his Colt .45 and shoot the blacksmith, who died the following day.

•Joe Grant: Billy killed Joe Grant January 10, 1880. Grant was said to be drunk. Grant was armed with an ivory handled pistol, which Billy inspected. He repositioned the chamber so that the next time it was fired it would be on an empty shell. Later, Grant got the nerve to draw and fire on Billy. Grant's gun merely went "click" and Billy shot him three times in the chin.

•James Bell: Bell was a deputy guarding Billy at the Lincoln County Courthouse. Billy shot him while escaping from the jail.

•Robert Ollinger: After killing Bell, Billy took a shotgun from the sheriff's gunroom and waited until Deputy Ollinger returned from dinner. Billy hated Ollinger from previous confrontations.

Chapter 2

Pearl Hart

Pearl was the last person—and only woman to rob a stagecoach.

Her story begins near Toronto, Canada where she was born about 1870. Pearl was a beautiful girl who had a penchant for dating a lot of men. Her promiscuous choices were not always the best.

At sixteen, Pearl married hot-blooded Frederick Hart, a gambler who lost more than he won. Hart physically abused his wife, and after five years, she left him, taking a train to Trinidad, Colorado.

When she arrived in Colorado, Pearl discovered she was pregnant and returned home to her family in Canada. After giving birth to her son,

Pearl was a promiscuous girl

Pearl left the child with her mother and headed west again, arriving in Phoenix in1885.

Frederick Hart followed her, begging her to come back to him. He promised he would get a regular job and they could start a new life together. Hart went to work as a

23

hotel manager, and for the next couple of years, the couple lived what is said to be somewhat of a wild life on Washington Street in Phoenix. Pearl gave birth to a second child, this time a daughter.

Wanderlust again caught up with Frederick Hart. He told Pearl he was tired of the domestic life, and joined Teddy Roosevelt's Rough Riders in Cuba. Pearl returned home to Canada with her daughter.

The West still pulled at her. She again left her family and headed for the Arizona mining camps, working at whatever jobs she could find to feed herself.

Eventually, she wound up in Phoenix, where she met Dan Bandman, a dancehall musician and tinhorn gambler. It was a bad relationship. Bandman taught Pearl how to drink, smoke, and even use opium. When Dan enlisted in the Spanish-American War his relationship with Pearl ended.

For a while, Pearl was eking out a living cooking for miners in a tent pitched along the San Pedro River in Mammoth, Arizona. Here, she met a miner who called himself "Joe Boot", probably an alias.

Boot convinced her they should move to Globe, Arizona where they could do better at mining. Joe's optimism was short-lived, as their mining claim was a bust.

Pearl Hart in "outlaw" Togs

To worsen Pearl's situation, she received a letter from her brother telling her that her mother was quite ill and

24

needed funds for medical bills. Pearl was desperate. She had no money, and no idea where to get any.

Joe came to the rescue. He concocted the idea of robbing the Globe to Florence stagecoach. This stage ran from Globe, Arizona to Florence, Arizona and it always carried passengers. Joe theorized, "These passengers carry traveling money and would be easy pickings."

Drawing their guns, Pearl and Joe jumped in front of the Globe stage and ordered the driver to stop. Henry Bacon, the driver of the stagecoach, carried a Colt .45, but not expecting to use it, on that day it was unloaded.

The days of Indian raids and stagecoach robberies were thought to be a thing of the past. In fact, the Florence-Globe line was one of the few remaining stagecoach runs that had not been replaced by the railroads.

Joe and Pearl stopped the stage as it was forced to slow while approaching a sharp turn at Cane Springs. Pearl was dressed like a man, but the swell of her bosom made it clear to the passengers that one of the bandits was a woman.

While Joe covered the driver, Pearl emptied the pockets and wallets of the three passengers. She took $380 from a salesman, $36 from a "tenderfoot" with his hair parted in the middle, and $5 from a Chinese traveler.

Pearl, who knew what it was like to be destitute, showed her compassionate side. She returned one dollar to each passenger so they would have something on which to eat.

Joe and Pearl were inept bandits and destined to be failures. They immediately became lost in the hills of Arizona. Neither had any experience with horses. They left such a trail that a Globe, Arizona posse soon found them.

Pearl's capture excited the town citizens who soon referred to her as the "Bandit Queen". They came to the jail to get her autograph or at least a glimpse of the new celebrity.

Sheriff W.E. Truman found Pearl's newfound fame annoying and shipped her to the Pima County Jail in Tucson. Her notoriety, however, continued to grow there. Newspaper reporters were beginning to sympathize with Pearl and her plight because of her explanations of why she participated in the robbery in the first place.

To stir up matters even more, Pearl insisted that she would never consent to be tried under a law that she or her sex had no voice in making. Pearl had become a strident voice for "women's emancipation" and believed women should have just as much right to vote as did men.

In the Tucson jail, Pearl formed an alliance with prison trustee Ed Hogan, who was allowed to roam freely throughout the jail. One night, Hogan cut a hole through the wall in Pearl's cell, and the two of them fled to Deming, New Mexico.

Again, Pearl's incapacity as an outlaw came through. She and Hogan were quickly arrested. On June 15, 1899, Pearl and Joe Boot both came up for trial. Joe pleaded guilty and was sentenced to 35 years in jail.

Not so, Pearl, even though she had boasted hundreds of times that she had been a part of the stagecoach holdup. She pleaded not guilty, a verdict the jury upheld.

This verdict enraged Judge F.M. Dean. He quickly had the bailiff re-arrest Pearl and berated the jury for its dereliction of duty. She was tried again on the charge of stealing the stagecoach driver's pistol.

This time, the jury gave her five years in prison. Pearl was sent to the Territorial Prison in Yuma, Arizona. On the trip there, some reports say, she smoked cigars constantly, and her puffing matched the smoke emitting from the train's engine.

With the arrival of Pearl, prison guards quickly shifted their attention from other prisoners to watch the outlaw queen. Newspapermen and camera fiends continued to seek interviews and snapshots.

Arizona's territorial governor pardoned Pearl Hart December 1902, two years before her sentence was up. The governor explained that the prison lacked accommodations for women prisoners.

Years later, Arizona historian Bert Fireman uncovered the real reason for the pardon. Pearl was pregnant, and the father would have had to be another prisoner or a prison guard.

Pardoning her allowed the prison to escape the scandal that might have ensued if her baby had been born in prison. A condition of the pardon was that Pearl would leave Arizona for good.

After Pearl's adventures and misadventures as an outlaw, one of her old school chums wrote the Arizona Historical Society, describing the "Bandit Queen's" teenage activities:

"She was a pretty girl and had a wonderful figure and voice. She could imitate a croaking frog, an owl, a hawk, and could sing like a mockingbird. She was lithesome, blithe, and witty, gushing with fun and jollity. She was also a wonderful dancer.

"She possessed one detrimental fault. She was too amorous, accepted too many dates with handsome young men, which finally caused her undoing."

Many rumors followed her release from prison. One is that she appeared on the vaudeville stage, reenacting her role as a lady bandit. Some say William Randolph Hearst bankrolled the show.

Another rumor is she joined the Buffalo Bill Wild West Show. Still another story is that Pearl headed a gang of pickpockets in Kansas City.

There is one story that says Pearl Hart married a cowboy named Calvin Bywater (in Mexico). They then went to live near the Dripping Springs Mountains, not far from Cane Springs where Pearl and Joe Boot had robbed the stagecoach.

Chapter 3

Bugsy Siegel

Benjamin "Bugsy" Siegel took what he wanted when

Bugsy Siegel

he wanted it without feeling any qualms about it.

As Siegel biographer Mark Gribben wrote, "In his mind, other people were there to be used by him, which he often demonstrated during his long record of robbery, rape and murder dating back to his teenage years."

One thing that Siegel detested was his nickname, "Bugsy". He preferred to be called Ben by his friends. If you weren't his friend, "Mr. Siegel" would do just fine.

Siegel grew up in a section of Brooklyn teeming with Irish, Italian and Jewish immigrants. This slum and disease-ridden section is where Benjamin Siegelbaum was born in 1902.

Ben vowed that he would rise above the station of his father, a Russian-born immigrant that raised five children on his earnings as a day laborer.

His racketeering days began early. As a teenager, Ben and his best friend, Moey Sedway, conjured up an extortion racket against street vendors. Ben would approach a vendor and ask for a dollar. When the vendor told him to scram, Moey would then splash the vendor's wares with kerosene and set a match to them.

When they next ask a vendor for a dollar, he usually paid up.

The next step for Ben was to form a protection scam. Vendors paid Siegel and Moey in return for stopping anyone else from pulling the same rip-off on them that Ben and Moey had.

Bugsy Siegel left home without finishing grammar school. He prowled the East Side at night with a band of tough, ruthless teenage boys. Said author Dean Jennings, in his book, "We Only Kill Each Other: the Life and Times of Bugsy Siegel", Bugsy often rolled drunks, burglarized lofts, and learned to be fast with both a gun and a knife.

While twenty years old, Siegel was arrested for raping a neighborhood girl. This event became the first entry in Bugsy Siegel's criminal record. The rape victim was later dissuaded from pressing the charge and the case was dismissed.

Siegel met another immigrant teen outlaw while running his protection rackets. Together, he and Meyer Lansky would build the national underworld's murder-for-hire squad.

It was Lansky who determined that if they were to compete against the Italians and the Irish mobs, it was necessary for the Jewish boys of his Brooklyn neighborhood to organize.

"I told little Benny that he could be my number two," Lansky said years later. "He was young but very brave. His big problem was that he was always ready to rush in first and shoot—to act without thinking."

What became known as the "Bugs and Meyer Mob" included such names as Abner "Longie" Zwillman, who later ran the rackets in New Jersey; Lepke Buchalter, the head of Murder, Inc.; Lansky's brother Jake; and a young boy named Arthur Flegenheimer, who later made a name for himself as "Dutch Shultz".

Much of the Bug-Meyer mob's income came from bootleg liquor. The mob not only hauled liquor for their own wholesale liquor business, but also supplied armed convoys for other groups trucking liquor between Philadelphia and New York.

The Bug-Meyer group became closely associated with Lucky Luciano and his right-hand man, Frank Costello. During World War I, while the rest of the world was fighting in Europe, the Bugs and Meyer mob and Luciano's were terrorizing pawnbrokers, moneylenders, and immigrant businesses with shakedowns and robbery.

Lucky Luciano

One report notes that Meyer asked Ben to check out a bank as a place in which to deposit their growing bankroll.

Benny Siegel returned, saying, "I'm not putting any money in there. Anyone could bust in and steal every dime in the place."

Two weeks later, the Bugs and Meyer mob did just that, escaping with eight grand.

Eventually, the Bugs, Meyer and Luciano mob looked for ways to tap into New York's illegal gambling market in New York. The gang started buying established bookmaking operations and to buy the protection of the police and politicians in New York's Lower East Side.

Joe "The Boss" Masseria and Arnold Rothstein, the recognized boss of New York's illegal gambling scene, didn't like the infringement of the Bugs and Meyer operation.

A crap game being operated by Bugs and Meyer was raided one night by a group of men who beat up the game's organizers, bodyguards and customers. The invading hoods told Lansky that this was only a warning. Unless the Bugs, Meyer and Luciano mobs paid tribute to Masseria and Rothstein, killings would follow.

Instead of caving in, they hunted down the Italian that led the raid on their gambling game. A huge fight ensued and the Masseria boys were beaten. By the time the fight ended, the cops arrived and Lansky, Siegel and some of their mob members were arrested.

The charge was disorderly conduct. The fine was two dollars.

More importantly, Masseria and Rothstein got the message that the Lower East Side belonged to the Bugs and Meyer mob.

When Prohibition ended, there was panic in the underworld. The golden goose for liquor runners and bootleggers was dead.

New York's special prosecutor Tom Dewey, who later ran for President of the U.S., was turning an eye toward Ben Siegel. It was at this time that Siegel decided to move to California.

He hated the name "Bugsy". He was tired of playing second fiddle to Lansky. He also wanted to mingle with the so-called respectable people without the threat of an embarrassing roust.

California and the western United States was almost untapped in terms of organized crime, even in the late 1930's. Jack I. Dragna headed the strongest gang in California. This was the Italian Protective League.

Bugsy and George Raft in 1944

In reality, the League was little more than a Mafia muscle outfit preying on the same immigrants it purported to protect.

Dragna's real name was Anthony Rizzoti. He held Charles "Lucky" Luciano in high regard. Luciano, at this time, was serving a 30 to 50 year jail term for prostitution.

Luciano sent word to Dragna that the Syndicate was moving to California. "Ben is coming west for the good of his health and all of us," Luciano told Dragna. He suggested that Dragna join with the syndicate or be taken apart by them.

While Dragna resented the intrusion, he decided to play ball. Even so, he did not like the interference of the Jewish gangster from New York and bided his time, looking for a chance to get rid of Bugsy.

Bugsy, his wife and their two daughters moved into a home Siegel rented from opera singer Laurence Tibbet. Ben also looked up George Raft, his old friend from his Bowery days, who had made good in the movies.

The two became regulars at Santa Anita Racetrack, wagering huge sums on the horses. It was Raft, too, who opened the door to Siegel's first West Coast racket. This was their infiltration of the extras' union. Bugsy, with his old friend Moey Sedway, began extorting money from movie moguls who needed extras to make their films.

Once Siegel and Sedway had control of the extras' union, they began working on the stars themselves. Ben would approach a highly paid actor at a Hollywood party and say, "I'm putting you down for $10,000 for the extras."

When the star protested, asking, "What do you mean?" Siegel would respond that the star would be unable to work on his next picture if the producer couldn't hire any extras.

Siegel is said to have received more than $400,000 in one-way "loans" from movie stars during his first year in Hollywood. These were the same people who were so desperate to have him at their parties.

Ben Siegel was convinced that the race wire service was the key to wealth and power. Siegel knew he could not take over the only existing such wire, the Continental Press Service, for which bookies were paying $100 to $1200 a week to get.

The gangster theorized that it would be more feasible to start up a competing service than it would be to take over the existing wire owned by James Ragen, Sr. in Chicago. Consequently, the Trans-America Service, with Siegel directing operations, was born, with funding and close connections to Al Capone and his Syndicate.

Bookmakers need a quick, confidential and reliable method of reporting winners of the thousands of horse races being bet on each day. In addition to track conditions, jockey changes, scratches and post times and results, the wire service provided bookies with up-to-the-minute betting odds.

Law restricted race results on the legal Western Union wire. Western Union was only allowed to send the results after the race was declared official. An objection by a jockey or a steward's inquiry could delay the results several minutes.

This would allowed unscrupulous bettors to take advantage of bookmakers by getting unofficial results of the race and placing a bet before the bookmakers got the official results.

When Ragen, the owner of Continental Press Service, was mysteriously gunned down in Chicago, that service folded. The Syndicate heaped praise on Siegel and his partners, Mickey Cohen and Jack Dragma.

In the next breath, however, the Syndicate informed the trio that it would now take over the take from the wires services.

Bugsy, who was making $25,000 a month from the wire service's Las Vegas operations alone, balked, and told the Syndicate to keep its mitts off the wire service.

"I am gonna run the wire here," he told friends back east, "And it is all mine." Even Siegel realized he was essentially daring the Syndicate to come and get him.

Bugsy began looking toward Las Vegas for opportunities. The Nevada Legislature had adopted legalized gambling in an effort to raise revenue. What interested Siegel most was the off-track betting on horse races in Las Vegas.

He tried to buy into a couple of established gambling casinos, without luck. Instead, he bought a controlling interest in Billy Wilkerson's plan to build a luxurious hotel, complete with individual air conditioners, tiled bathrooms, and two swimming pools.

According to author Mark Gribben, Siegel wanted to build an oasis in the desert where travelers from both coasts would come for sun, fun, gambling and entertainment.

Ben called his dream "The Flamingo". From the start, things didn't go well. Bugsy was a gangster, not an architect, and some of the builders on the project were stealing him blind.

The original $1.2 million price tag soon spiraled to $6 million. The mob's treasury was near dry and many of the individual mobsters who invested in the hotel were now deep in debt. Siegel kept going back to his Hollywood friends to get more money, with the promise, "You're in on the ground floor of the biggest gold mine in the world."

Author Gribben wrote that a conference of mobsters, including Meyer Lansky, Frank Costello, Luciano, Vito Genovese and Joey Adonis, met in Havana, Cuba. Lansky contended Ben Siegel had been skimming money from the mob and putting it in numbered Swiss bank accounts.

Luciano is quoted by the author as saying, "There was no doubt in Meyer's mind that Bugsy had skimmed this dough from his building budget, and he was sure that Siegel was preparing to skip as well as skim, in case the roof was gonna fall in on him."

When one of the mobsters asked Lansky what should be done about Benny, he answered: "There's only one thing to do with a thief who steals from his friends. Benny's got to be hit."

The Syndicate was unanimous in its approval. Assigned to do the task was Charlie Fischetti. But before Fischetti was to act, Meyer wanted him to wait until the Flamingo opened to see if the venture would make money. The opening date was set for the day after Christmas.

Meyer owed Benny any number of personal debts for his loyalty since their days in the New York slums. Luciano told a Siegel biographer, "Benny had been a valuable guy for a long time, almost from the beginning with me and Lansky and Costello, so none of us really wanted to see him get it. But if the Flamingo was a flop, that would be it for him."

The opening event was a disaster despite the array of Hollywood movie stars brought to the scene. Among the guests were such luminaries as Clark Gable, Lana Turner, Joan Crawford, Anne Jeffreys and Caesar Romero.

George Jessel was emcee, and entertaining the crowd was Rose Marie, George Raft and Jimmy Durante. Xavier Cugat's orchestra provided the music.

The Los Angeles weather did not cooperate. Two Constellations chartered to bring Hollywood stars to the event could not take off because of fog. In Vegas, a steady rain fell.

There were not yet any hotel rooms available at the Flamingo when it opened. Consequently, casino winners took their winnings to the Frontier in downtown Las Vegas to spend the night. Most of the celebrities brought to the Flamingo for the grand opening left after the second day.

When Siegel admitted that the opening had been a flop, the gangsters again assembled in Havana and gave the order for Fischetti to fulfill his assignment. Lansky again came to Siegel's rescue, urging the mob to wait.

He, like Siegel, believed Las Vegas could be tapped for profits. He suggested a delay. The Flamingo would be put into receivership to stop the losses, he explained, and then the mob could move in and buy out the legitimate partners for pennies on the dollar.

Bugsy shot in mistress' apartment.

Siegel was allowed to close the Flamingo until the hotel was finished, with a grand reopening planned for March. This time, Benny came away a winner, with the hotel resort reporting a profit of $250,000 for the first half of 1947.

Benny began to relax again. While lazily reading newspapers at the bungalow he shared with his mistress, Virginia Hill, a fusillade of shots crashed through the living room window.

Bugsy was struck in the head, blowing one eye fifteen feet from his body. Four more shots were fired from a 30-06 weapon, breaking his ribs and tearing up his lungs. Bugsy Siegel was dead at 42 years of age.

Chapter 4

Joaquin Murrieta

The legend of Joaquin Murrieta becomes stronger as the years pass. To most "Joaquin" fans, he was not a villain at all, but a proud Mexican avenging the wrongs thrust on him and his encampment. Thereby hangs the tale of Joaquin Murrieta, considered one of California's most notorious bandits.

Joaquin Murietta

In 1848, there were two rival gold camps, one at Angel's Camp and the other at San Andreas. The San Andreas mine was founded by Mexican prospectors, led by Joaquin Murietta, and it turned out to be a rich mine.

American miners considered the Mexicans an inferior race and not worthy of such a rich claim. Twenty-one American miners from the Angel's Camp mine poured into the camp of San Andreas, driving the Mexican miners out.

When the fiery tempered Americans descended on Murrieta's camp, they hung Joaquin's half-brother Jesus for a crime he had not committed. They also horsewhipped Joaquin and raped the outlaw's girlfriend,

Mariana. (Some say her name was Rosa and that she was married to Joaquin)

This incident so outraged Joaquin, he took to the outlaw trail. He became one of the West's most talked about outlaws. Joaquin became a legend equal to another notorious California bandit at that time, Tiburcio Vasquez.

There is a difference between the two banditos, however. There are police records to authenticate the many crimes of Tiburcio Vasquez, but no such records exist on Joaquin Murrieta.

Joaquin formed a band of cutthroats to prey on American settlements after the death of his brother and the ravaging of his girlfriend Mariana. Joaquin and his gang traced down and eventually brought all 21 Americans involved in murdering his brother to justice. Joaquin himself is said to have dispatched 19 of them.

Some historians consider Joaquin a myth, created in the fertile brain of newspaper reporter John Rollin Ridge, who, in 1854, wrote what was designated as "The Life and Adventures of Joaquin Murietta". Ridge was a part-time miner, auditor, recorder, deputy county clerk, poet, and newspaper writer.

There are some who say Joaquin's half-brother Jesus was still alive and living in Mexico in the 1860s.

Whichever story holds true, Joaquin was considered the most notorious bandit in the Mother Lode Country. To his Mexican brethren, he became something of a Robin Hood of the West.

Joaquin's first outlaw escapade was to dispatch the killers of his brother. The wanton killings aroused the Calaveras community. They held mass meetings, passing resolutions in which all Mexicans were ordered to leave the county. At the same time, civilian posses scoured the region for the outlaws.

At one point, three Mexicans, supposedly part of Joaquin's band, were unceremoniously hanged, proof or no proof. Bands of Americans drove the Mexican population from San Andreas and the upper Calaveras River.

A Stockton newspaper account reported, "If an American meets a Mexican, he takes his horse, his arms, and bids him to leave." In another story, the Stockton Republican said, "No man dare travel a step unless armed to the teeth or sleep without having a firearm already in his grasp."

As the pressure against all Mexicans increased, Joaquin and his band decided to head north. They robbed as they went. At one point, they attacked a Chinese camp, massacring six people and making off with $6,000.

Three of the Murrieta band were captured near Fiddletown and forced to depart on a single horse, two riding and the other running behind while hanging onto the horse's tail.

There is one story printed in the March 1, 1972 issue of the "Los Altos Town Crier" noting that Joaquin may have hidden some gold loot in what is now a pet cemetery.

Joaquin and seven of his band had held up some wayside taverns in Hayward and in Newark in 1851. They escaped with the loot toward the southwest. When they crossed the Guadalupe River, eyewitnesses claimed the bandits still were carrying stolen money with them.

They rode down Foothill Boulevard past the proposed site of the pet cemetery on what was then the Mountain View-Stevens Creek Road. When the gang reached the intersection with the Cupertino stage trail, Murietta and his men no longer had the loot.

It is believed they buried the gold in a little glen destined to become a pet cemetery.

Atrocities laid at the hands of Joaquin and his gang continued, angering government officials as well as residents. Finally, Governor John Bigler authorized Captain Harry Love, a former Mexican War express rider, and now a California peace officer, to take 20 rangers and bring Joaquin to justice.

Love was given three months to catch Joaquin and his band of outlaws. The rangers caught up with Joaquin and his band near the town of Coalinga.

The Murrieta gang was ensconced in its stronghold, the Arroyo de Cantua, a haven of caves and rocks, with palisades of massive buttes knows as Tres Piedras, or "Three Rocks."

In the ensuing battle, Joaquin was killed. The ranger who fired the fatal shot at Joaquin was William Henderson. To prove the deed was done, Love and his rangers carried back the head of Joaquin, along with the deformed hand of "Three-Fingered Jack", a member of the Murrieta gang.

Both the head and the hand were preserved in a keg of brandy (although other accounts say it was a pickle jar). The head was exhibited in a San Francisco museum, which was later destroyed in the Great Earthquake and Fire of 1906.

Some accounts maintain that Joaquin's fierce mustache continued to lengthen as the head floated in the jar over the years.

Other skeptics insisted the head in the pickle jar was not that of Joaquin at all. These doubters pointed to the fact that Joaquin was comparatively light complexioned, showing a high degree of Spanish blood.

The head in the brandy appeared to be of an older man with a swarthy complexion. History never truly determined that it was indeed the head of the bandit. Some, who claimed to have known Joaquin back in Calaveras County, said the head was not that of Joaquin at all.

Adding to the claims of the doubters, it was duly noted the pickled head was never placed on exhibit in Calaveras County where he would have been more readily recognized.

Fiction writers have muddied the Joaquin Murrieta waters even more over the years, adding their own figments of imagination to "el bandido magnifico", the Bandit of the El Dorado.

As historian Angus MacLean said in his book, "Legends of the California Banditos," it is just as well that Joaquin's true escapades remain unknown. "It is doubtful if the real-life Murrieta could ever have been as intriguing as the legendary one."

Contributing to the doubts that Murrieta ever existed are the variations in spelling of his name by various historians, alternating between Murrieta and Murrietta with an extra "t", as well Murieta, with a single "r", as it was in Ridge's 1854 book.

The name of his girlfriend, too, has been variously listed as Rosita, Rosalisa, Carmela, Carmen, Clarinda, Clarita, and Mariana.

Back in 1853, there were reports from Americanos in El Pueblo de San Luis Obispo that Joaquin and his band rode into the little town, forcibly taking over the mission gardens and campground.

The townspeople were so convinced it was Murietta, they hid in the basement of a store, staying off the streets for two or three days until the outlaw band moved on. Joaquin Murrieta's capture and death is supposed to have happened July 25, 1853.

Detractors of Ridge's book point out there are little in contemporary accounts to substantiate the tale of Joaquin Murrieta. It is noted, as well, that few newspaper reporters at the time had much chance to obtain first-hand information for their papers.

The saga of Joaquin Murrieta seems more placed in word-of-mouth accounts than in solid, written records. Some versions passed down in the folklore say that Murrieta, recognizing the futileness of his cause, gathered up his loot and headed for Mexico. Some old-timers even claimed to have seen him in later years.

There are some tales that traitors in his outlaw band had put Joaquin to a grisly torture death some weeks before Harry Love's rangers claimed to have found and killed him.

This version has been attributed to Mariana Murietta, the "widow" of Joaquin. Often called Mariana La Loca by her fellow townsmen, she was said to willingly tell different versions of Joaquin's death in exchange for money.

Further, she often stated, it was she that had found the mutilated body of Joaquin, the head still intact, which she buried near a tree in Cantua Canyon.

Joaquin's outlaw career, if true, covered less than three years and he was little known outside his own small circle of confederates. Whatever the truth, Joaquin Murrieta has survived, becoming a folk hero in both California and Mexican lore.

Chapter 5

The Dalton Gang

The Dalton Brothers weren't always on the outside of the law. For a short time, Frank Dalton, the oldest of the brothers, was commissioned a deputy marshal for the federal court in Fort Smith, Arkansas. He was killed in a gun battle with the Smith-Dixon Gang.

The three younger Daltons also had early connections on the good side of the law. Grat Dalton, who had moved to California with his brother Bill, returned to Indian Territory, where he, too, worked as a deputy.

Grat received a bullet wound in his arm while attempting to arrest one suspect. He was later commissioned a deputy marshal for the Muskogee court.

Bob Dalton

Bob Dalton, the more famous of the brothers, was a deputy marshal for the federal court in Kansas in Wichita. He also served on several of his brother Frank's posses.

Emmett Dalton earned his living working as a cowboy on the Bar X Bar Ranch near the Pawnee Agency. There

47

he met Bill Doolin and William St. Power, alias Bill Powers, alias Tom Evans.

The Dalton brothers soon figured they could earn more money stealing horses and cattle than they could working as lawmen.

Bob, Grat and Emmett Dalton, in July 1890, were accused of stealing horses near Claremont Indian Territory and selling them in Kansas. With a posse in hot pursuit, Bob and Emmett left the territories for California. Grat was arrested and jailed, but released for lack of evidence. He joined Bob, Emmett and Bill in California

The four Dalton brothers attempted to rob A Southern Pacific Railroad train in the little San Joaquin town of Alila, California (now known as Earlimart). The robbery was botched, but a fireman on the train was killed. The Daltons were blamed for his death.

Grat was caught and jailed on charges of attempted robbery. Bob and Emmett somehow escaped and fled back to Oklahoma. While awaiting sentence, Grat, too escaped and made his way back to Oklahoma.

Grat Dalton

The Dalton Gang adopted train robbing as their chosen profession. Other hardcore outlaws, including Charlie Bryant and Bitter Creek Newcomb, joined the Gang. In May 1891, the gang, headed by Bob Dalton, decided to rob a train at Wharton, in the Oklahoma Territory.

Some accounts claim that U.S. Marshal Chris Madsen was aboard, and the Dalton Gang knew it. The gang went car-to-car searching for him. Madsen escaped being killed by jumping from the back of the train and hiding in the darkness.

The train pulled out before he considered it safe to get back on board, and Madsen was left staring as the train disappeared down the tracks. The Dalton Gang ended up with $1745 in cash from that robbery.

At Adair, in Indian Territory, eight members of the Dalton Gang made its last train robbery on July 14, 1892. As the train approached, four men ordered the night operator at the station to "flag down" the train.

As the train slowed to a standstill, two members of the gang boarded the engine while the others covered the conductor and trainmen. The station operator was taken to the express car where he ordered the messenger inside to open up.

When the messenger refused, the train's fireman was ordered to break open the door with his pick. Once inside, the bandits were quick to rifle the safe and its contents.

The train was loaded with deputies, but the gang was so quick and quiet with their activities that the lawmen didn't know the train was being robbed until the job was virtually over.

Deputies did engage in a short but fierce gun battle, during which an innocent bystander was killed. The bandits escaped with an unknown amount of cash.

The Dalton Gang was feeling intense pressure from lawman. Heck Thomas, one of the most fearless lawmen in the service of the U.S. government who pursued the

Daltons. He pressed them, never letting them stay in one place for long.

He trailed them into the Osage Nation and, on October 3rd, 1892, located their hideout, but the brothers had already fled. He picked up their trail, and followed the gang as they moved toward Onion Creek just outside of Coffeyville, Kansas.

Bob Dalton is believed to have been jealous of the notoriety of Jesse James and his gang. He wanted to pull a robbery that would put him in the same lofty category as Jesse James.

Bob and his brothers decided one last robbery would get them enough money to flee the country. Bob Dalton's plan was to rob two banks in the same city at the same time.

His reasoning was that the robberies would provide enough money to finance their escape into Mexico, and two such robberies in the same city at the same time had never been done before and would therefore be unexpected.

What the Daltons didn't figure in was the fact their faces were well known to everyone in town. Even their fake beards and mustaches provided little disguise. During that bank raid, a 10-minute gun battle ensued. Eight men were killed and four were wounded.

Even before Heck Thomas reached Coffeyville, he received news that the Daltons had been killed during the bank raid. He hurried into Coffeyville and identified the bodies for the Wells Fargo Company.

Killed in the raid were both Grat and Bob Dalton, along with gang members Bill Power and Dick Broadwell. Injured, and not expected to live was Emmett Dalton.

Emmett did eventually recover and served seventeen years in prison.

After his release, he wrote about his story, and lived the remainder of his life in California.

In his book, "When the Daltons Rode", written in collaboration with Los Angeles newspaperman Jack Jungmeyer, Emmett noted that men slipped rather easily from one side of the line to the other. "Reformed outlaws sometimes made good officers—and sometimes good officers became outlaws."

According to the book, the Dalton's troubles started when Bob, Emmett, and three of their friends were riding through New Mexico en route back to the Indian Territory.

They rode into a mining camp and sat in on a faro game. They lost heavily. They were convinced the game was crooked. They pulled their guns and took back what they had lost plus a bit more.

According to Emmett's book, the Dalton Gang never numbered more than 10 men. Later, there were scores who claimed to have been members of the gang.

Chapter 6

Bill Doolin

Bill Doolin first rode with the Dalton brothers before forming his own group called the "Wild Bunch". None of the outlaws of the Old West can compare to the cunning of the bandits who invaded the Twin Territories of Oklahoma and the Indian Nations.

Doolin's first brush with the law, before joining the Daltons, came when he and several other cowboys decided to throw a party in Coffeyville, Kansas. The cowboys sawed barrels in half, and filled them with beer and ice.

Bill Doolin

Kansas was a dry state, and this party didn't sit well with the sheriff. When the sheriff and his deputies confronted the cowboys, there was a shootout, and two officers were wounded. From that moment on, Bill Doolin was an outlaw.

William "Bill" Doolin was born in 1858 in Johnson County, Arkansas. When he turned 23 years old, he drifted west and went to work for Oscar D. Halsall of Texas on his ranch on the Cimarron River in Oklahoma.

It was while working as a cowboy on Halsall's Oklahoma ranches that Bill Doolin met most of the

53

members of his future "Wild Bunch." Among them were George "Bitter Creek" Newcomb, Charlie Pierce, Bill Power, Dick Broadwell, Bill "Tulsa Jack" Blake, and Emmett Dalton.

Soon after his confrontation with the law in Coffeyville, Kansas, Doolin began riding with the Dalton Brothers. He participated in several train robberies with the Daltons.

When Bob Dalton and his brother Grat were killed in a failed double-bank robbery in Coffeyville, Kansas. Bill Doolin assumed control of the gang. There is considerable confusion among historians as to why Doolin was not along on that fatal bank raid.

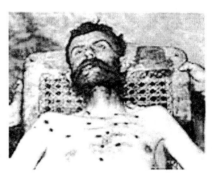

Bill Doolin, dead from buckshot.

Bill Doolin and his Wild Bunch were riding high by the spring of 1893. Not only was their reputation growing, but also their deeds were becoming bolder.

The Doolin gang would wantonly shoot at anyone or anything that might get in the way of their robbery. Innocent bystanders often became their victims.

Doolin married Edith Ellsworth on March 14, 1893. Whether Edith knew that Doolin was an outlaw at the time of the wedding is not known. It is known that throughout his outlaw career, she stuck by him.

After the Dalton Gang was wiped out at Coffeyville, there were still three members of that gang left. These include Bill Doolin, George "Bitter Creek" Newcomb, and Charlie Pierce.

Doolin's Wild Bunch is believed to have made its first train robbery just seven days after the Daltons were killed at Coffeyville. The Coffeeville Journal gives no names for the robbers, but the blame was laid on Bill Doolin and his Wild Bunch.

One heavily armed member of the robbery gang boarded the train as it pulled out of Caney, Kansas. The robber worked his way to the engine, and order the engineer to stop the train about two miles out of town.

The fireman and engineer were then ordered to cut the engine and the baggage car from the rest of the train and proceed another half mile up the track.

When the robbers ordered Express Messenger Maxwell to open the door, he refused, even when told the car would be blown up with dynamite. It took begging by the engineer and fireman to get the messenger to open the baggage car door. The robbers got away with $1,500 that night.

Two more gang members, Oliver "Ol" Yantis and Richard "Little Dick" West, joined Doolin's gang. The gang's first robbery with their new additions was the Ford County Bank at Spearville, Kansas. To confuse the townsfolk, "Little Dick" West galloped up and down Main Street, yelling and shooting into buildings to panic everyone. The gang got away with $4500.

By the end of the year, Doolin added even more members to his gang. It now included Bill Blake (alias Tulsa Jack), Richard Clifton (alias Dynamite Dick), George Waightman (alias Red Buck), William "Little Bill" Raidler, and Mason Frakes "Bill" Dalton.

It was about this time that two teenage girls became enamored of the Doolin Gang. Annie McDoulet, alias "Cattle Annie", and Jennie Stevens, alias "Little

Britches", first met members of the gang at a country-dance.

Cattle Annie was completely infatuated with Red Buck and would have done anything for him. The girls did not take part in the robberies, but they did play a handy role acting as spies and messengers. They could also drive the stolen horses and peddle whiskey.

The gang received a new member in the summer of 1893. Nineteen-year-old Roy Daugherty (alias Arkansas Tom Jones) signed on after becoming acquainted with some members while working as a cowboy.

The sheriff had learned the Doolin Gang often rode into the little town of Ingalls, just east of Stillwater, Oklahoma, to spend some of their stolen money. The Lawmen planned a grand play to capture the outlaws.

Thirteen deputies stuffed into two covered wagons with plenty of guns and ammunition. The wagons pulled into town and deputies were dropped off at prime spots. Marshal John Hixon assigned the men to strategic locations so that the outlaws could be arrested when they tried to leave town.

The plan went awry, however, when Bitter Creek Newcomb left his friends in the saloon and went outside to look around. Deputy Dick Speed recognized him and opened fire. Arkansas Tom, lying sick in his hotel room, heard the commotion and drilled the deputy.

When that fracas was over, three deputies were dead, two innocent bystanders died and another wounded. Both Doolin and Bitter Creek were wounded. Arkansas Tom was captured when he ran out of ammunition. The rest of the gang got away.

The Doolin Gang robbed a bank in Pawnee, and later a railroad station in Woodward. In Southwest City,

Missouri, the Wild Bunch almost suffered the same fate as the Dalton Gang at Coffeyville.

Law officers and citizens both took up arms against them and they had to shoot themselves free every inch of the way to escape. Doolin received a buckshot wound in the forehead, but the gang escaped with fifteen thousand dollars.

Doolin began feeling queasy about the size of the gang. He thought the wise move would be to split up, meeting now and then at prearranged places. Bill Dalton and four others formed the Bill Dalton Gang. They robbed the First National Bank in Longview, Texas.

An innocent bystander was killed during their getaway. Lawmen tracked Bill Dalton to his hideout in Indian Territory. Deputy Lawson Hart killed Bill Dalton in a shootout.

The last robbery the Wild Bunch pulled as a gang was at Dover, Oklahoma Territory. There, they boarded the Rock Island train and robbed the express car.

Unaware a posse was hot after them, the gang headed west and camped at Ames. Deputy Marshal Chris Madden and his posse caught up with them about two o'clock in the afternoon. In a shootout, Tulsa Jack Blake died.

The rest of the gang scattered. They would never again re-unite as a gang. Soon after, Bitter Creek Newcomb and Black Face Charlie Pierce were killed in a setup, and their bodies turned in for the $5,000 reward.

Bill Doolin offered to surrender to Marshal Evett Dumas "Ed" Nix in exchange for a light sentence. Nix refused the offer. With so many of his friends now dead, Doolin joined with his old gang member Little Dick West and headed for New Mexico.

This pen and ink drawing done by Bob Meldrum in 1914 depicts James W. Davis, bartender, shooting Jeff Dunbar in a barroom brawl. The "Wild Bunch" were frequent visitors to the saloon in Dixon, Wyoming. *(Wyoming State Museum)*

Doolin missed his family. He now had a two-year-old son, as well as a bum leg from the shootout in Cimarron, Kansas two years earlier.

Marshal Bill Tilghman was on his heels. When Tilghman learned that Edith Doolin had disappeared from Lawson, Oklahoma, where she lived with her parents, he was sure it was to reunite with Doolin.

The lawman tracked Doolin and his wife to a small camp thirty miles northeast of Arkansas City, Kansas, a place where Doolin was unknown but which knew well. Doolin soon learned that Tilghman hunting him.

In the dead of night, he left his wife and child behind to get Tilghman off his trail. The lawman, it is said, spent many wasted days watching Edith, hoping Doolin would reappear.

Tilghman learned that Doolin had been treated for rheumatism, and one of the places the doctor had discussed with the outlaw was the sulfur baths in Eureka Springs.

When Tilghman reached Eureka Springs, one of the first men he saw was Bill Doolin. Doolin was using the alias of Tom Wilson. Tilghman arrested Doolin and brought him back to Guthrie to stand trial. He accomplished the arrest without a shot being fired.

Eight days after Dynamite Dick was brought to the Guthrie jail to join Doolin, the two desperados escaped, taking eight prisoners with them. Because his injured leg hampered his activities, Doolin headed for his old haunts along the Cimarron River.

Deputy Heck Thomas and his posse cornered Doolin heading out of town with all his belongings loaded in a wagon. When Doolin opened fire on the posse, he died from twenty buckshot wounds in his chest.

His body was dressed and placed on exhibition in Guthrie, Oklahoma where hundreds of people viewed it. Doolin was laid to rest in the Boot Hill section of Summit View Cemetery in Guthrie.

60

Chapter 7

Belle Starr

Belle Starr was most likely a "tom-boy". She had two older brothers and three younger ones. Her parents were John and Elizabeth Shirley. Named Myra Maybelle Shirley when she was born in 1848, her family called her "May".

As a child, May had a hot temper and was ready to fight anyone who crossed her. Her mother sent her to the Carthage Female Academy where she studied to be a lady, as well as languages, reading, writing and arithmetic.

Belle Starr

May adored her older brother Bud. The two spent a great deal of time riding the hillsides near the hotel their father owned in Carthage, Missouri. Bud instructed Belle in the use of firearms, and she became expert with both pistol and rifle.

Missouri at the time was a Civil War battleground, split by the issue over slavery. Belle's father owned slaves, and the Shirley family was on the side of the Rebel forces.

May was proud when her brother Bud joined Quantrill's Raiders, a squad of bushwhackers using bloody reprisals to fight the Union Army. May was only fourteen, but she wanted to help in the war effort.

Unable to fight because of her gender, May became a spy for the Rebels. She learned how many men the Union Army had at various encampments, the kinds of guns they had, and other information she passed on to the Rebels.

In 1864, a unit of Union soldiers killed her brother Bud, a captain in the Rebel Army. May vowed to avenge her brother's death though it's not known that she ever did.

John Shirley had enough of the

Belle Starr riding sidesaddle

fighting between the states. He and his family packed their belongs on two covered wagons and headed for Texas, where Preston, the oldest of the Shirley boys had a farm near Dallas.

The Shirley family, including May, settled on a farm in Scyene, Texas, near Dallas. It was well known that in 1866 Cole, Jim, Bob and John Younger, along with Jesse James, used the Shirley home as a hideout. Some historians claim May's first lover was the outlaw Cole Younger.

There is some question when May started calling herself Belle, which she preferred. She had become enamored with a Jim Reed back in Missouri.

When Jim's family followed the Shirleys to Texas, it did indeed please Belle, and the two hastily resumed their romance. One story says that Jim and his friends carried Belle off on horseback, and they held a hasty wedding while still on their horses. The ceremony was performed by one of the men in the party rather than an ordained minister.

Belle's relationship with Cole Younger is the subject of many stories.

One tale claims that Cole was the father of Belle's daughter, Rosie Lee. Cole denied it, and it is most likely that the father of Rosie was Jim Reed. Belle married Reed November 1, 1866, and Rosie Lee, later called Pearl by her mother and friends, was born two years later.

When her husband Jim became bored with farm life, he began spending more time in the Indian Territory where he gambled and raced horses. He became friends with Tom Starr, the head of a large family that held little respect for the law.

Jim Reed was never far from trouble. When his brother was murdered in Arkansas, Jim followed and shot the killers. This deed placed a murder charge on Reed. He hurried back to Missouri to pick up Belle and their young daughter. The three sought safety with Tom Starr.

Belle and her husband later moved to Los Angeles, where May, who had by now adopted the name Belle, gave birth to a son she called James Edward.

Jim Reed was arrested in Los Angeles for passing fake money. This arrest led to police learning about the murder charge against him. He jumped bail and headed east. Belle, Pearl and little Eddie followed by stagecoach.

When they arrived in Texas, Belle's father gave the couple a farm. Before long, this farm became a hideout for horse thieves. Reed continued his outlaw ways by torturing and robbing Watt Grayson, a rich farmer, escaping with $30,000.

Some tales say that Belle participated in the robbery, dressed as a man. No member of the Grayson family, nor their hired hands who had witnessed the robbery, mentioned a woman dressed as a man, or even a slightly built man.

Belle left her husband and moved back to her parent's house, but spent part of her time in a Dallas hotel. She soon became known as the "Bandit Queen", a name she accepted eagerly, for she was having a good time spending Jim's stolen money.

When Jim took up with a new girlfriend and a new outlaw game, Belle broke off the marriage. Jim continued his outlaw ways, robbing stagecoaches, looting mail sacks, and stealing livestock. A large reward was put out for the capture of his gang.

Lawman John Morris followed Reed to Paris, Texas, caught the outlaw off guard and shot him, collecting a $1,700 reward. The event also left Belle a widow and destitute. The next few years of Belle's life are something of a mystery.

There are writers who have suggested a number of illegal activities that Belle participated in during this period, but there is little documentation attesting to these claims.

For instance, she is accused of burning down a store, robbing a bank, being jailed for horse stealing, and then eloping with her jailor. She is accused of robbing a poker game at gunpoint, running a livery stable, and fencing livestock.

Still other rumors say Belle lived for a brief time with Bruce Younger, the uncle of outlaw Cole Younger. Author Phillip Steele, in his book, "Starr Tracks: Belle and Pearl Starr," says Belle and Bruce Younger were married in Chetopa, Kan., on May 15, 1880.

Yet other records show that on June 5, three weeks later after the supposed marriage to Younger, she married Sam Starr.

Belle, it is said, liked men, and men liked her. She especially liked big men, and Sam Starr, the son of Tom Starr, was a big man.. He was six feet five inches tall. A handsome Cherokee, Sam was nine years younger than Belle, when they were married in a tribal ceremony.

Belle and Sam claimed one thousand acres of Indian land forty miles west of Fort Smith, Arkansas, which she called "Younger's Bend. Most of the couple's friends were outlaws, and their farm soon became a hideout.

Jesse James, Belle said, was her first guest. While holed up at Younger's Bend, the outlaws kept busy stealing horses, robbing salesmen and selling whisky to the Indians.

Belle sat in on meetings of the outlaws and helped plan new robberies, and she bought and sold stolen horses.

These activities caused lawmen to come to Younger's Bend. A U.S. marshal charged Belle and Sam with stealing a horse valued at $80. He arrested them and took them to Fort Smith for trial.

When convicted, Belle and Sam feared what their sentence would be. The judge hearing their case was

65

Isaac Parker, who had sent eighty-eight men to the gallows. His sentence for Belle and Sam, however, was somewhat light. He gave them one-year terms in a Michigan prison.

Soon after Belle and Sam returned home, Sam was accused of robbing a store and post office. With police on the lookout for him, he went into hiding. Three months later, Belle herself was accused of stealing horses again. At her trial, she produced a witness who swore that Belle had paid a stranger $50 for the horse and she was released.

Sam wasn't faring so well. Feeling somewhat safe one day, he went riding on Venus, the best horse in Belle's stable. A four-man posse led by Frank West, an old enemy of Starr's, opened fire. One bullet killed Venus, and another grazed Sam's head.

When two of the posse members went to get a wagon, Sam was able to grab a rifle. He disarmed the two remaining posse members and escaped on one of their horses.

At Belle's urging, Sam turned himself in to a lawman that took him to Fort Smith. Belle rode behind the two men with pistols strapped to her waist. After Sam was charged, she put up his bail.

A week before Christmas, the Starrs went to a dance at a neighbor's house. During the party, Sam was informed that Frank West, his old nemesis, was outside. Sam confronted West, accusing him of killing Belle's horse Venus.

The confrontation led to both men drawing their weapons. While Sam fired first, West was also able to draw. Both men lay dead.

Belle loved her outlaw husband, and his death crushed her in more ways than one. Sam's death meant that she could not keep her farm, as only Cherokees could live on Cherokee land. Belle would have to move unless she could find a new man.

On Sam's death, there are some reports that say she returned to Younger's Bend and took notorious outlaw Jack Spaniard to her bed "almost before Sam's body was cold". This arrangement was cut short when Spaniard was arrested, tried for murder, found guilty and hanged.

She then invited Tom Starr's adopted son, Bill July, to move in with her. Even though 15 years younger than she, with him by her side, her farm was safe. At the same time, she announced that outlaws were no longer welcome at Younger's Bend.

Belle turned forty in 1888, but looked much older with her sun-weathered face and her hair now streaked with gray.

One story told about Belle is the day her hat fell off when she was riding her horse in Fort Smith. A cowboy who saw the hat fall refused to pick it up. Belle pulled her Colt .45 and ordered him to pick it up.

When the cowboy obeyed, she took the hat and said, "The next time a lady asks you to pick up her hat, do as she tells you."

Belle was arrested three times—twice for horse theft and once for arson. She was convicted on one theft charge. There are no records of Belle ever killing anyone.

Belle and her husband, Bill July, began renting portions of their property to people wanting farming acreage. One, Edgar A. Watson, came to terms with Belle, paying her cash for the rent.

When Belle became friendly with Watson's wife, she learned that Edgar Watson was wanted for Murder in Florida. Belle was too well aware of the tribal council's threat to expel her from her land if she were caught harboring fugitives again.

She attempted to back out of the rental arrangement with Watson. The renter insisted he would farm the land for which he had paid.

In a face-to-face confrontation, Belle told Watson that Florida authorities might be interested in his whereabouts. The furious Watson accepted the refund of his money and settle on another farm in the vicinity.

On February 22, 1889, Belle and her husband Bill July, went to Fort Smith, she to shop and he to a hearing on a horse stealing charge against him. After finishing her shopping, Belle stopped at the house of some neighbors, the Jackson Rowes.

The home was a popular gathering place for members of the community. One visitor there was Edgar Watson, the renter with whom Belle had quarreled. Soon after Belle's arrival, Watson left.

As she returned to Younger's Bend, she traversed the road that passed within several hundred yards of Watson's place. She was suddenly blown from her saddle by a shotgun blast.

When Belle's daughter Pearl saw her mother's horse showing up rider-less, she set out to find out why. Pearl and neighbors arrived at Belle's side before she died, but Belle was unable to utter any last words.

Belle's husband Bill July and her son, Eddie, both accused Watson of killing her. Watson was arrested, but the only evidence against him was termed circumstantial.

He was released and soon left the area along with his wife.

No other attempts were made to find the murderer. However, there were some other potential suspects, among them, July himself. It is said that July had been caught playing around with a young Cherokee girl, and Belle had been making his life hell.

A few weeks later, a deputy who was on his trail mortally wounded July.

Belle Starr is buried near Eufair Lake, southeast of Porum, Oklahoma. On her tombstone is engraved a horse, along with the following words:

> She not for her the bitter tear,
> Nor give the heart to vain regret
> Tis but the casket that lies here,
> The gem that filled it sparkles yet.

Chapter 8

Black Bart

Black Bart's method of operation was different from other bandits of the day. Bart was no ordinary ruffian. He planned and executed his robberies with careful research and undeniable finesse.

Bart's legend begins at a desolate spot in Calaveras County along the Sonora-Milton stage run. The stage was nearing the top of Funk Hill at the head of Yaqui Gulch. The date was August 3, 1877.

There, a lone highwayman, wearing a long white duster and a flour sack over his head, stepped out in front of a stagecoach. He pointed a double-barreled shotgun at the stage driver.

In a terse, four-word instruction, the bandit gave his order: *"Please throw down the box."*

It was while robbing a stagecoach on the Point Arena-Duncan Mills route that the robber first got the pseudonym Black Bart. The bandit worked alone and left few clues for lawmen to follow. In the box thrown down to the robber was about $300 in coins and a check for $305.52. The check was never cashed.

The box was later found empty, except for a bit of poetic doggerel.

The poem read:

I've labored long and hard for bread—

For honor or for riches—
But on my corns too long you've tred,
You fine-haired sons of bitches.

It was signed "**Black Bart, the Po8.**"

While Black Bart's bit of poetic tomfoolery and clean getaway may have caused howls of delight to those who read about the event, rest assured that Wells Fargo officials were not amused.

Wells Fargo offices up and down California were put on lookout for this robber-poet.

In his robberies, he wore a unique mask. Over his head, he wore a flour sack with eyeholes cut in it, atop of which was perched a derby hat.

Over what appeared to be rough miners clothing, he wore a soiled linen duster. He covered his boots with heavy woolen socks, apparently to distort his footprints.

"Please throw down the box," Bart would order the driver. While he collected all the loot

Black Bart.

from the strong boxes, Black Bart never bothered to take the valuables of the passengers

When one panicked lady tossed him her purse, Black Bart handed it back to her with the reply, "Thank you madam, but I don't need your money. I only want Wells Fargo's."

Black Bart's first stage robbery occurred near Funk Hill, four miles outside of Copperopolis. The driver of the stagecoach, John Shine, who was later a U.S. marshal and a California state senator, tossed Bart the wooden box reinforced with iron bands.

The outlaw grabbed the box and hurried into the trees. Being a curious person, stage driver Shine drove a short distance, stopped his stage, and then walked back to the scene of the robbery. He soon was staring into a half-dozen guns leveled at him from behind boulders.

Shine stood rock still. He then realized the outlaws were not moving. When he approached one, he found it was simply a dummy with a stick for a gun. This became a usual method for Black Bart.

He would stop a stage, pretending to have an outlaw gang supporting him. Bart would shout, "If he dares to shoot, give him a solid volley, boys!"

Stage driver Shine told Wells Fargo agents and Calaveras County Sheriff Benjamin Thorn that one thing stood out about the bandit. "He was extremely polite."

Black Bart used a number of Aliases, including Charles F. Bolton and Charles E. Boles, which police believed to be his true name.

Wells Fargo posted a reward: The poster stated: "REWARD! Wells Fargo & Company's express box containing $100 in gold notes was robbed this morning by one man, on the route from Sonora to Milton, near the top of the hill between the river and Copperopolis. $250 and one-fourth of any money recovered will be paid for the arrest and conviction of the robber."

Black Bart soon began changing his robbery tactics. He would use darkness to help hide his identity. He became known as being one of the few highwaymen to commit stage robberies at night. But Wells Fargo Agent Jim Hume believed that highwayman was getting bolder. He was no longer taking the precaution of wearing socks over his boots.

In one empty strong box, this piece of poetry was found:

> *"Here I lay me down to sleep*
> *To wait the coming morrow.*
> *Perhaps success, perhaps defeat*
> *And everlasting sorrow.*
> *Yet come what will, I'll try it once,*
> *My conditions can't be worse,*
> *And if there's money in that box,*
> *Tis money in my purse."*

While he robbed, Black Bart didn't rob frequently. There was often as much as nine months or even a year between holdups. He later told lawmen he "took only what was needed when it was needed."

Bart always cut the mailbags open, using an inverted T shape slash. After one robbery, a Wells Fargo agent who observed the T-shaped slash said, "He might as well have signed his name."

Black Bart's absence from the stage runs didn't deter others from holding up the stagecoaches. Robberies became serious enough at one time that Wells Fargo officials said they might discontinue the stage runs.

While Bart held up stages as far north as the Oregon border, he concentrated his efforts in the gold country of the Sierra Nevada. From the time of his first holdup,

Black Bart was credited by lawmen with stopping 28 stages over an eight-year period.

To say the least, the bandit had local sheriffs, Wells Fargo detectives and U.S. Postal authorities in a fiery rage. He always stopped the stagecoaches while they were traveling along mountainous roads where the driver was compelled to slow down at dangerous curves.

On November 3, 1883, the Sonora stage was rolling along toward Copperopolis, carrying a lone passenger. The passenger was a young boy with a rifle, who told the driver he wanted to do some hunting. He asked the driver to pick him up on the other side of the hill.

When the boy disappeared, Black Bart appeared, and confronting the stage driver, giving his usual order, "Please throw down the box." Wells Fargo had adopted a new tactic. The company began chaining the box to the floor of the stagecoaches.

Bart ordered the driver to take the horses up over a hill while he worked on the box. While it took the highwayman longer than usual to open the box, he did get it loose by pounding it furiously with his hatchet. He pulled out a knife, slashed the sacks, and extracted the registered letters before telling the driver to move on. The opened letters were found the next day in a nearby ravine.

As the driver was doing so, he met the boy with the rifle coming round the hill. The two hurried back as Black Bart was scrambling into the brush with the loot. The boy sent three shots at the outlaw, wounding him in the hand.

Bart used a handkerchief to wrap around his wound. Lawmen later found the bloodied handkerchief, which had a San Francisco laundry mark on it. One of the detectives assigned to track down Black Bart was Henry Nicholson Morse, one-time sheriff of Alameda County.

Morse faced an arduous task. He had the robber's handkerchief with the laundry mark, FX07, but he soon learned there were ninety-one laundries in San Francisco. He was determined to visit every one of them if necessary.

At Ferguson and Bigg's California Laundry, Morse struck pay dirt. He found the laundry mark belonged to Charles E. Bolton, a mining engineer. Morse arrested Bolton in his hotel room, but when booked, Bolton gave his name as T.Z. Spaulding

In the hotel room, detectives found a Bible that had been given to a Charles E. Boles by his wife in 1865. Born and raised in upper New York State, Boles had been a farmer, and later served as a sergeant in the 116th Illinois Volunteer Infantry just before the Civil War. The lawmen's investigation left them assured that it Boles who was the much wanted Black Bart.

When Boles' family members had died, he had headed to California where he briefly panned for gold and worked a few other odd jobs before turning to stagecoach robbery.

Records show that Black Bart (Boles) had invested his loot in several small business ventures that provided him a modest income. As money would become short, however, he would return to stagecoach holdups.

For days after his arrest, Boles denied being the famous Black Bart. He finally did admit to several robberies, but only those occurring before 1879. He mistakenly believed he was protected by the statute of limitations for those holdups.

Black Bart was finally convicted January 21, 1888. He was sentenced to six years in San Quentin. This was shortened to four years for good behavior. By the time of his release, he was aging considerably, with both his eyesight and his hearing beginning to fail.

As he left the prison, his spirit seemed crushed. He hurried to escape the newsmen that surrounded him when he stepped from the prison gates.

Boles, alias Black Bart, disappeared after his release and was never heard from again.

There was a report that he may have returned to holding up stagecoaches. While it was never proven, some thought it was Bart that robbed a Wells Fargo stage on November 14, 1888. The lone bandit in that holdup left a note that read:

> *"So here I've stood while wind and rain*
> *Have set the trees a sobbin'*
> *And risked my life for that damned stage*
> *That wasn't worth the robbin'.*

When carefully examined by Wells Fargo detective James B. Hume, however, the note was declared a hoax and not the work of Black Bart. Humes said he was sure that Black Bart had permanently retired.

This declaration brought on speculation that Wells Fargo may have pensioned off Black Bart after his departure from prison on the condition that he not rob any more stages.

Black Bart was reported in New York newspapers to have died in 1917, something that was never confirmed. Before that, Detective Hume had received a report that the outlaw had died in the high California mountains while hunting game.

While the outlaw had gained considerable fame for his stage holdups, it should be remembered, he never fired a shot.

Chapter 9

Jesse James

The two James brothers and the four Younger brothers were a unique half-dozen. All six of the men held grudges against the union and fought hard to retain slavery during the Civil War. They decided to surrender when the Civil War ended in order to escape the firing squad.

As the James brothers and the Younger brothers rode north to Lexington to surrender, a member of a Union troop they met on the way shot Jesse, even though he carried

Jesse James

a white flag to show he was unarmed. His chest wound was serious, bringing him near death.

Jesse recuperated at the home of his mother and stepfather in Nebraska. They had moved there to escape being harassed because of their sympathy for the south. Jesse's wound was slow to heal and Jesse wanted to return to Missouri. He did not want to die in a Northern state.

He traveled by steamboat to Kansas City where his cousin Zee Mimms nursed him back to health. When well enough to travel, Jesse returned to the old Samuel place, owned by his mother and stepfather.

Jesse had no intention of becoming a farmer. As days went by, friends from his war days dropped by. Like Jesse, none were looking for honest work.

The war and guerilla fighting had taught Jesse and his friends some hard lessons. From those lessons, Jesse conceived the idea of robbing banks and living a high life from the loot.

Jesse Woodson James was born in Clay County, Missouri on September 5, 1847. He and his brother Frank, as well as Cole Younger, were Confederates in the Civil War, trained in guerilla fighting by one of the best, William C. Quantrill.

Jesse was only 15 years old when he joined Quantrill's Raiders. Frank James and Cole Younger were also with Quantrill when, in August 1863, the town of Lawrence, Kansas was hit and one hundred eighty two citizens were murdered. Jesse and Frank James's war experience taught them to fight. As confederate soldiers they were essentially outlaws.

Jesse James as Quantrill Raider

When they turned to bank robbery, the James brothers seemed to always disappear into thin air, confusing sheriffs, U.S. marshals, the Pinkerton detectives, and citizen posses. They were constantly hunted during their sixteen-year reign of terror from 1866 to 1882.

According to Jesse James biographer Robertus Love, in his book, "The Rise and Fall of Jesse James", Jesse would have like to have gone straight again. The story goes thus:

Jesse met the pastor who preached at his church as a boy. The old pastor asked, "Jesse, why don't you stop these things you're doing?"

"If you'll tell me just how I can stop," Jesse replied, "I'll be glad enough to stop, but I don't intend to stop right under a rope."

When the minister replied, "Well, anyhow, you ought not to forget your religion, Jesse. I'm sorry you've forgotten your bringing-up. Get back to your religion."

With that, Jesse withdrew a small book from his inside-coat pocket. He handed it to the minister.

"It was a copy of the New Testament," the minister later recounted. "I looked through it and was astonished. Never in my life have I seen a Bible so marked up, showing such constant usage."

The first bank robbery blamed on the James-Younger band was in Liberty, Missouri at the Clay County Saving Association Bank. The date was February 13, 1866. It is said to have been the first bank robbery ever held during daylight hours.

On that morning, Greenup Bird, cashier, and his son William, bookkeeper, came to work. Two bandits entered the bank while others held watch outside. One bandit covered the senior Bird, while the other stood watch over the son.

"Open the vault or I'll blow your head off," the elder Bird was ordered. Wanting to keep his head intact, he complied.

After scooping up the contents of the vault, one robber, believed to be the joke-loving Jesse, said, "All birds should be caged. Get in the vault," he ordered Greenup and William Bird.

The bandits got away with sixty-two-thousand-dollars. Forty two thousand of this was in bonds, five hundred-eight dollars was in U.S. Government Revenue Stamps, and the rest was in gold, silver coins and greenbacks. One man was killed during that robbery.

It was eight months before another bank was robbed in Missouri. Five horsemen rode into Lexington at noon, when many of the town's businessmen were closed for lunch and the bank was deserted.

Cashier J.L. Thomas, having nothing to do during the slow period, stood in the doorway of the bank, chewing a quill toothpick. He watched the five horsemen dismount and tie their horses in an adjacent alley. As two of the men headed toward the bank, Thomas returned behind his counter, anticipating some banking business.

One man presented the cashier with a fifty-dollar bond, asking if he could cash it. As he counted currency from the cash drawer, the other four horsemen appeared.

"Now give us all the money you have in the bank," the man who asked for change ordered. "Do it quietly and quickly and you won't be hurt; but if you don't, you'll get your head blown off."

The five horsemen rode out of town calmly, carrying two thousand dollars.

It was four months before the daylight bank robbers made their third raid, this time on the private bank of Judge McLain in Savannah. The robbery, like the Lexington holdup, was at 12-noon.

Judge McLain and his son were in the bank when four of the five strangers entered. The suspicious McLain slammed the safe door shut, snatched his pistol from under the cash counter, and began firing. McLain received a bullet to the throat as his son rushed into the street, announcing the bank was being robbed.

The robbers left without a penny of banker McLain's money. As with the other robberies, residents quickly labeled the culprits. "The James gang again!" was the hue and cry.

The next hit was in Richmond in Ray County, Missouri. This was the bloodiest of all the bank raids led by the James-Younger outlaws. The gang had grown in number. Instead of five, some counted as many as fourteen men in the robber gang.

The men were all mounted on fast horses. While some dashed about issuing their Rebel guerilla yell, six others dismounted at the Hughes & Mason Bank. They broke into the bank, which was closed at the time, and crammed about four thousand dollars into their customary burlap sack.

In the melee, the mayor of Richmond was killed. The outlaws then tried to free several Confederate sympathizers from the Richmond jail. The jailor and his fifteen-year-old son were killed.

These killings so outraged citizens that warrants were issued for eight of the men that were identified as part of the gang.

The James brothers and Cole Younger, who was suspected of being a gang member, presented good alibis. It is noted others presented the airtight alibis, as the James boys and Cole Younger were discreetly hidden.

Pinkerton detectives were getting closer to the James-Younger outlaws. For nearly a year, the group stayed in hiding. Then, in March 1868 the outlaws struck, not in Missouri, but in Kentucky.

The quiet little Logan County town of Russellville was the target. In that holdup, six men rode into town, wounded

Jesse James home where he was shot

two people, and rode out with fourteen thousand dollars.

Jesse James was a hunted outlaw with large rewards hanging over his head. The decade from 1871 to 1881 was a bloody and active period for the James gang. The Youngers stayed with the James boys through half of that decade before dropping out.

Missouri had become known as "the Robber State." Missouri land prices were down because of the outlaws robbing of trains and banks. Soon the gang branched out into other states.

A gang descended on Wayne County, Iowa. They thought the bank at Corydon, in the middle of the Hog and Corn Belt, should be easy pickings. There is no evidence that Jesse James and his cronies were involved in this episode.

This didn't deter the public from assuming it had to be the James-Younger crew. The James's and Youngers had become quite adept at devising air-proof alibis. They would name many persons in their home counties that could testify to their presence in Missouri at the time the Iowa bank was robbed.

In Kansas City, a different type robbery occurred that was generally blamed on Jesse James and his gang. The robbery occurred at the Kansas City fairgrounds where the famed trotter, Ethan Allen, was racing.

About 4 p.m. the treasurer at the fair counted the proceeds, placed the money in a lock box, and gave it to a young courier to take to the bank. Just as he stepped outside the fairground gate, three horsemen rode up.

One of the horsemen dismounted, grabbed the cashbox from the courier, handed it to one of his mounted partners, and remounted. They rode away, firing many shots.

The next robbery accusation against the James gang was far from previous robberies. This occurred in Ste. Genevieve, where the first white settlement on Missouri soil was made. The town consisted of Roman Catholics of French extraction.

It was not unusual for as much as one hundred thousand dollars to be on hand in the Ste. Genevieve Savings Association. Ste Genevieve was located far from Jesse James territory and seemed relatively safe from such a gang.

When the five robbers converged on Ste. Genevieve, the group split. Two men rode in from the north and three from the south. O.D. Harris, cashier, and Firman A. Rozier, Jr. the son of the bank's president, were the only people in the bank.

The bank was in the process of liquidation and most of the one hundred thousand dollars the bandits expected had been shipped to St. Louis. The robbers got only four thousand dollars for their efforts. Much of it was in silver coin.

The coin sack was so heavy that the bandit carrying it dropped the bag when his horse stumbled. The whole party halted while he dismounted to pick up the loot.

But when the bandit attempted to remount, the unwieldy sack struck against his horse's flank. The coins made such a clinking sound the horse bolted and bounded back toward Ste Genevieve. An unknowing farmer traveling along the road to town caught the horse and returned it to the outlaws.

The first railroad train robbery was attributed to the James-Younger gang. The first train robbery occurred in Iowa. The gang learned there was to be a big gold shipment from the West to the East by way of the Chicago, Rock Island & Pacific Railway.

The holdup was planned to take place a few miles west of Adair, Iowa, where a sharp curve presented an excellent opportunity for wrecking the train. The seven robbers tethered their horses in nearby woods, and removed a spike from a rail.

They left the loosened rail in place but tied a long rope to it. Two of the robbers, lying in shrubbery and grass a few yards from the track, held the other end of the rope.

Even though the engineer had seen the rail move suddenly to the outside, his efforts to stop the train failed. The locomotive plunged off the track, turning on its side, crushing the engineer to death.

The seven outlaws boarded the train and ordered the messenger in the express car to open the safe. They got a measly three thousand dollars for their effort. They did get several hundred dollars from the passengers.

Ironically, twelve hours later, an express train carrying seventy-five thousand dollars in gold passed safely eastward over the replaced rail. The advance men who gathered the information for the gang had made a miscalculation in time.

Pinkerton detectives were hot and heavy on the trail. They were intent on bringing an end to the outlawry. One thing that chewed on their soul was that during the eight-year reign of the outlaws, not a single James or Younger had been caught, killed, or even wounded.

A young Pinkerton agent named John Whicher showed up in Liberty, bragging he was going to get Jesse and Frank James. His plan included getting a job on the Samuel farm so he could spy on Jesse. A few days later, the agent's body was found near Kearny, Missouri, shot through the heart.

Jesse and Frank was so wanted that one bank offered $3,000 for their capture. A railroad added another $5,000 to the reward. This high reward money brought the Pinkerton agents back into the hunt.

In 1875, nine Pinkerton detectives sneaked up on the Samuel farm. Two sweaty horses in the barn told them that Frank and Jesse were probably in the house. The detectives tossed a kerosene bomb in the fireplace.

Dr. Samuel tried to kick the bomb into the fireplace. He was too late. It went off, killing nine-year-old Archie, Jesse's brother, and injured his mother, Zerelda. Her arm had to be amputated.

Someone opened fire from an upstairs room. One of the Pinkerton agents was wounded, dying a few days later. Missouri Governor Thomas Crittenden vowed to rid the state of the outlaws. He added $5,000 reward for their capture.

Jesse married his cousin, Zee, who had nursed him back to health from his earlier wound. They had a son, Jesse Edwards James. The outlaw wanted to settle down.

Adopting the alias, J.D. Howard, Jesse moved his wife and son to Waverly, where he joined the church and sang in the choir. After two years, the money from his holdups ran low.

He despised hard farm work. He decided to organize a new gang. Frank James refused, saying he was tired of the outlaw life. Word went out that Jesse was looking for new men; he soon recruited five promising members.

The new gang robbed a train in Glendale, Missouri. Jesse gave each gang member his share of the six thousand dollars taken, and returned home to Nashville. No one there suspected the quiet Mr. Howard of being a part of that holdup.

Frank James had a change of heart. He decided to rejoin Jesse and his newly formed gang. Jesse had a new plan. They would rob a train, but this time the gang would buy tickets on the train they planned to rob.

With the gang all on board, Jesse pulled his pistol and shouted a signal. Everyone froze, but Jesse fired anyway, killing the conductor. The gang forced their way into the rail mail car and cleaned out the safe.

Everything was going wrong for Jesse, it seemed. The gang got only eight hundred dollars from that robbery, but had killed two men. Jesse's brother Frank was also discouraged. He went back to his farm. He and Jesse never saw each other again.

When Jesse struck again, it was to rob a bank in Platte City. He figured he could do the job with three men. He recruited Charlie and Bob Ford to pull off the robbery.

While no one knows the whole story, it is believed that Bob Ford took his brother Charlie aside, and suggested they kill Jesse for the reward money. Charlie agreed.

On April 3, the Fords joined Jesse and his wife Zee for breakfast. After eating, the men moved to the living room, and Jesse removed his guns. Jesse climbed onto a chair to adjust a picture that had drooped to one side.

Bob Ford's bullet hit Jesse in the back of the head. He was dead when he crashed to the floor. Bob and Charlie were sentenced to death for their crimes. But Governor Crittenden kept his word and gave the men who killed him a full pardon for bringing down the most famous outlaw in history.

Chapter 10

Turbicio Vasquez

By the time he was 21-years-old, Tiburcio Vasquez led his own gang of bandits. Even at this young age, he was well on his way to becoming California's master outlaw.

Vasquez, like his contemporary, Joaquin Murietta, was a California legend. But unlike Murietta, who had no police records to document his outlawry, Tiburcio Vasquez was well known on police blotters.

Tiburcio Vasquez

From his early background, Vasquez should never have been a bandit. He was born to a respected family in Monterey on August 11, 1835 (some sources list his birth date as 1839). The Vasquez home was a handsome adobe structure located behind Colton Hall, where California's first Constitutional Convention was held, and which still stands today.

Some historians claim Vasquez got his first push down the road to outlawry through his association with Anastacio Garcia, reputedly a one-time member of the Joaquin Murietta band of outlaws.

Vasquez centered his outlaw activity on the wagon routes leading from Los Angeles to the Cerro Gordo Mines and in the San Joaquin Valley. His final capture was in what is now West Hollywood.

It seems unlikely that Tiburcio would become an outlaw. As a young man, he attended school in Monterey and learned to read and write with proficiency, an accomplishment he was justly proud of all his life.

It was one night in 1852 that Vasquez launched on his criminal career. While attending a *fandango* in Monterey with Anastacio Garcia, Vasquez became embroiled in a melee in which Constable William Hardmount was slain. The young Tiburcio fled to the hills with Garcia.

Vasquez claimed his crimes were the result of his hate for the *Norte Americano* who had discriminated against Californians of Spanish and Mexican origin. He hated the gringos for leveling slights and insults at his family origin.

By 1856, Tiburcio had his own gang and was soon considered California's master outlaw. Vasquez specialized in the stealing of horses, making a series of raids on ranches from Monterey County to Los Angeles. The Vasquez gang would rebrand and sell the stolen horses.

After rustling a herd of horses from a ranch near Newhall in Los Angeles County, Vasquez tried to sell them too soon. A sheriff's posse caught him and a companion. When his companion turned state's evidence, Tiburcio was sentenced to five years in San Quentin.

He continued his outlaw activity after his release from prison. Vasquez joined with two other infamous California *bandidos,* Tomas Redondo, alias Procopio or Red-Handed Dick, and the bloodthirsty villain Juan Soto.

Their crimes ranged from Sonoma County south into the San Joaquin Valley. Vasquez was in and out of San Quentin three times.

In 1873, Vasquez and his *desperado* companions went too far. In a raid in Tres Pinos, a small town six miles south of Hollister in San Benito County, three citizens were killed and two hundred dollars in gold was stolen.

News of this murderous escapade made Vasquez a household word throughout northern and central California. Governor Newton Booth offered a thousand-dollar reward for the apprehension of Vasquez.

The bandit realized that northern California was now too hot for him. With two trusted companions, Clodovio Chavez and Abdom Leiva, Vasquez headed south. Near Buena Vista Lake, Abdom's wife, Rosaria Leiva, joined the trio.

The group headquartered at Heffner's Ranch, nestled among the pines near tiny Elizabeth Lake in the Antelope Valley.

It was no secret that Vasquez considered himself a ladies' man. And his amorous intentions toward the comely Rosaria Leiva almost brought about Vasquez's demise.

Abdom Leiva suspected that something was going on between Vasquez and his wife. When he returned early one day, he found the two in a *"fragrante delicto"*, or sexual embrace.

The enraged Abdom drew his pistol and threatened to shoot Vasquez. Clodovio Chavez dissuaded him from doing so, and Leiva left the camp with his wife, vowing vengeance against Tiburcio at some later time. Leiva left his adulterous wife at the ranch.

True to his word, Leiva rode to Lyon's Station in Soledad Canyon where he surrendered to authorities and readily agreed to turn state's evidence against Vasquez. With the sheriffs of both Monterey and Los Angeles County in hot pursuit of them, Vasquez and Chavez managed to escape.

But with information supplied by Leiva, several Vasquez gang members who had remained in hiding in San Benito and Monterey counties were apprehended.

Vasquez came out of the mountains long enough to get Rosaria at Heffner's ranch. The couple, along with the faithful Clodovio Chavez, rode back into the San Gabriel Mountains. During the time of their seclusion, Rosaria became pregnant.

The outlaw could not stand the weeks of inactivity. In 1873, Vasquez decided to leave his mountain haunt and organize a new outlaw band. The presence of the pregnant Rosaria was now a hindrance to the outlaw.

He abandoned her in the mountains, where she was alone and helpless, dispelling any thinking that the bandit was a gallant Robin Hood type folk hero.

Rosaria was later able to make her way out of the wilderness and eventually to her home in San Jose.

On the day after Christmas, 1873, Vasquez and his gang made front-page news by sacking the town of Kingston in Fresno County. They bound victims and relieved them of their valuables, and looted two stores, taking twenty five hundred dollars in cash and jewelry.

This act enraged the sheriffs of Fresno, Tulare, San Joaquin, Santa Clara and Monterey counties, who all organized posses to hunt the Vasquez gang.

The California legislature empowered Governor Newton Booth to spend fifteen thousand dollars to bring

Vasquez to justice. In 1874, the governor offered a reward of three thousand dollars for Vasquez alive or two thousand dollars for him dead. A month later, these figures were raised to eight thousand alive and six thousand dead.

Sheriff Harry Morse of Alameda County, capturer of Juan Soto and a host of other desperados, was assigned the task of tracking down Vasquez. With a handpicked posse of deputies, Sheriff Morse set out.

The robber band fled, eventually arriving at the stage station in Coyote Holes. There they fired several shots into the roof and ordered the occupants out. Their victims were lined up, robbed of their valuables, and marched behind a nearby hill and tied up.

Then the gang waited for the late arrival of the Owens Valley stage bound for Los Angeles. Vasquez expected to find a fortune in the strongbox, but instead found only $10,000 in mining stock. This he simply scattered to the wind.

Sheriff Harry Morse continued on Vasquez' trail. His break came when Vasquez went to rob sheep rancher Alexander Repetto, who had recently sold a large quantity of wool. When Vasquez and his band drew pistols, Repetto could only produce eighty dollars.

The puny sum enraged Vasquez. The outlaw then ordered Repetto to write a check for $800. Repetto's thirteen-year-old nephew was then dispatched to take the check to the Temple and Workman bank in Los Angeles and bring back the cash.

While Vasquez had warned the lad that his uncle would be killed if he informed anybody of the gangsters' activity, bank officials nevertheless became suspicious over the youth's nervousness. The officials notified Sheriff Billy Rowland.

The sheep man's nephew had scarcely handed the money over to Vasquez when the outlaw spotted the dust of Sheriff Rowland and his posse. He and his gang again departed for the hills. During the chase, Vasquez' horse stumbled into a steep gully, breaking a leg. Vasquez jumped aboard the horse of another gang member and again escaped the law.

But the outlaw's luck was running out. Vasquez made a fatal mistake after the Repetto incident by not fleeing to Mexico as his friends had urged him to do.

Law officials, still on Vasquez tail, learned that the bandit was hiding in the Cahuenga Mountains (now Hollywood Hills) at the ranch of Greek George. It is believed a former gang member gave the information to the sheriff.

Los Angeles sheriff Billy Rowland dispatched a deputy by the name of D.K. Smith to stake out Greek George's ranch. Disguised as a *vaquero* looking for work, Smith hung around the ranch for several days before he finally spied Vasquez.

This set in motion the actions leading to the capture of the notorious outlaw. The sheriff commandeered a wagon driven by two Mexicans going into the mountains to gather wood. Six deputies hid in the bed of the empty wagon and the Mexicans were ordered to drive up to the ranch house of Greek George.

Vasquez had just settled down for lunch. He sprang to his feet as armed deputies burst through the door. The bandit made a flying leap through the kitchen window into the drawn pistol of George Beers, a reporter for the

San Francisco Chronicle who had been allowed to accompany the lawmen.

Vasquez spent nine days in the Los Angeles jail and became the object of statewide attention. In interviews granted to three reporters, Vasquez continued to insist he had never killed a man and that his motives had always been honorable.

In the eight months preceding his trial, Vasquez was transported to the jail in Salinas and charged with the murder of Leander Davidson at Tres Pinos. He was then moved to San Jose to stand trial.

Vasquez continued to be something of a celebrity and even a hero to hundreds of his fellow Spanish-speaking citizens. He seemed to enjoy his notoriety, even autographing and selling photographs taken after his arrest.

His trial for murder was held in January 1875. The trial lasted four days and the jury took two hours to reach a guilty verdict. He met his death by hanging on March 19, 1875, in San Jose.

Vasquez' loyal lieutenant Clodovio Chavez, fled to Yuma, Arizona. He was shot to death there by two deputies.

The outlaw is still remembered by two place names in southern California. Vasquez Canyon, the Big Tujunga tributary used by the outlaw in his getaway, immortalizes the Repetto Ranch raid. Vasquez Rocks, above Soledad Canyon, is now a Los Angeles County park, and marks one of the bandit's favorite hideouts.

Chapter 11

Doc Holliday

Doc Holliday, said lawman Wyatt Earp, "...was the most skillful gambler, and the nerviest, fastest, deadliest man with a six-gun I ever saw."

This indeed is great praise for a man who studied dentistry and occasionally practiced his craft. He is said to have been a good dentist, but learned soon after starting his practice that he had contracted tuberculosis.

Doc Holliday

He contacted a number of doctors, but most agreed he had only a few months to live. He was told to seek a drier climate. In 1873, Holliday packed his bags, boarded a train, and got off in Dallas, Texas, the end of the railroad line.

While he did hang out his dentist shingle, his coughing spells caused by his tuberculosis forced him to curtail his practice. He would break out coughing during the most embarrassing moments, such as in the middle of filling a tooth or during the extraction of one.

Holliday had a talent for gambling. This quickly became his sole means of support. Because of the hazards involved with being a professional gambler, he practiced long and hard in shooting and knife skills.

The only thing faster than Holiday's draw was his temper.

When, after a provocation, Holliday put two shots into a Dallas citizen, he was forced to flee Dallas, steps ahead of a posse. He stopped at the tough little cow town of Jacksboro, in Jacks County, where he took a job dealing Faro.

Holliday now carried a gun in a shoulder holster, another one on his hip, and a long wicked knife. In a short span of time, he became involved in three more gunfights. In one, he left a man dead. No legal action was taken against him.

He then became so careless that he killed a soldier from Fort Richardson. The U.S. Government jumped into this investigation, and Holliday, knowing he would be stretched by a rope if caught, was forced to flee. He headed for Apache country in Colorado.

The hot-tempered Holliday seemingly could not stop getting involved in arguments. He killed three more men before he reached Denver.

Doc had traveled west knowing he had a short time to live. Actually, the drier climate added an extra fifteen years to his tortuous, tubercular existence.

Eventually, Doc Holliday ended up in Fort Griffin, Texas. There he met the only woman ever to come into his life. She was called "Big Nose" Kate. She was a dance-hall girl and prostitute and had a temper that matched that of Holliday..

It was in John Shanssey's saloon where Holliday met both Big Nose Kate and lawman Wyatt Earp. Earp rode into town in search of train robber Dave Rudabaugh. Doc helped Earp gain some of the information he needed for Rudabaugh's arrest and they became friends.

Doc seemingly could not avoid trouble and he never ran away from it. One day, a would-be tough guy named Ed Bailey sat down in a poker game with Holliday. To irritate Doc, Bailey kept picking up the discards and looking through them.

"Don't do that," Holliday warned, noting it was against the rules of western poker and anyone scanning the discards would forfeit the pot. When Bailey did it again, Doc reached across the table, and, without showing his hand, raked in the pot.

Bailey brought a six-shooter from under the table while Doc brought out a large knife. Before Bailey could pull the trigger, Doc had slashed his belly open. Thinking he was right in defending himself against the card cheater, Doc allowed the marshal to arrest him.

He had miscalculated because when Holliday was disarmed and locked up, Bailey's friends clamored for Holliday's blood. Big Nose Kate knew she had to do something quick or Doc was finished.

She swung into action by setting fire to an old shed. It burned rapidly and threatened to engulf the town. The only three people that didn't rush to fight the fire were Doc, his guard, and Kate. When Kate saw the guard and the prisoner alone, she stepped in with a pistol in each hand. She disarmed the guard, handed another pistol to Doc and they flew away in the night.

When they arrived in Dodge City, they registered at Deacon Cox's boarding house as Dr. and Mrs. J.H.

Holliday. Kate gave up prostitution and quit inhabiting saloons. Doc hung out his shingle again.

Finally, Kate told Doc she could no longer stand this dull existence and went back to the saloons and a life of prostitution. Doc went back to dealing Faro in the Long Branch saloon.

Doc was known to consume as much as four quarts of whiskey in a day. Sometimes, he would drink a pint before breakfast. This was the only medicine that seemingly relieved his tubercular cough. Still, most said he never appeared drunk.

When a number of Texas cowboys came into town with a herd of cattle, word arrived at the Long Branch that several of the trail drivers had cornered Wyatt Earp and intended to shoot him down.

Gun in hand, Doc leaped through the barroom door. He found two cowboys holding cocked revolvers on Wyatt, goading him to draw before they shot him down. Other cowboys stood by, taunting and insulting Earp.

"Pray and jerk your gun," roared Morrison, "your time has come, Earp."

Another voice rang out behind Morrison.

"No, friend, you draw or throw your hands up," said Doc Holliday, with his pistol at Morrison's temple. "Any of you bastards pulls a gun and your leader here loses what's left of his brains." The armed cowboys dropped their guns.

Shouting a stream of profanities, Doc distracted the cowboys long enough for Wyatt to rap the leader over the head with a pistol, then set about relieving the other cowboys of their guns.

Wyatt never forgot the fact that Doc Holliday had saved his life that night.

After another fight with Kate, Doc drifted out of town, locating in Trinidad, Colorado. There, a young gambler known as "Kid Colton" badgered Doc into a fight. Doc's hot temper flared, he fired twice and Colton lay dead in the street.

Doc headed out of town again, this time landing in Las Vegas, New Mexico. He opened a dental office again, but the new try at being respectable didn't work.

He then got into an argument with Mike Gordon, a popular man among the locals. Not hesitating, Doc invited him to start shooting when he was ready. Gordon was killed by three shots into the stomach.

Again, Doc had to get out of town in a hurry. He decided to go back to Dodge City, where he knew he would be safe, since Wyatt Earp there was his friend.

When he arrived in Dodge City, however, he found Earp had taken a lawman's job in Tombstone, Arizona, where he intended to meet with his brothers, James, Virgil and Morgan.

There was a nest of outlaws in Tombstone that deemed the town as their private domain. They didn't like the arrival of the Earp brothers, nor of Doc Holliday.

Included among these outlaws, known locally as the "Cowboys", were Ike and Billy Clanton, Frank and Tom McLaury, and Johnny Ringo. The "Cowboys" threatened to kill the Earps and Doc Holliday if they didn't get out of town.

As everyone in Tombstone knew, neither the Earps nor Holliday would run. Virgil received word that the Cowboys were gathering at the O.K. Corral and that they were armed, which was against City law.

Doc met the Wyatt, Morgan and Virgil Earp on Fourth Street on their way to the O.K. Corral. Doc insisted on going with them where five armed men, all potential killers, waited.

The fight at the O.K. corral was short-lived. Wyatt Earp and Billy Clanton started the battle. Wyatt shot Billy in the chest. He then cut Tom McLaury down with a double charge of buckshot.

A bullet from Frank McLaury cut into Doc's pistol holster and burned a nasty crease across his hip. Doc's return fire smashed into McLaury's brain.

The fight lasted less than 30 seconds. Virgil Earp had been shot in the leg, Morgan through both shoulders. Only Wyatt had emerged from the fight unscathed.

Doc Holliday's health was failing fast. He finally went to Glenwood Springs, Colorado to try the sulfur baths. His health was too far-gone. He spent his last fifty-seven days in bed, delirious fourteen of those days.

One morning, he awoke clear-eyed and asked for a glass of whiskey. He drank it down quickly, and, looking at his bare toes sticking out at the end of the bed, said, "This is funny". He died without his boots on at 35 years of age.

Chapter 12

John Wesley Hardin

One account says John Wesley Hardin was so mean he shot a man for snoring too loud. Hardin went wrong at an early age, and he always claimed he had never killed anyone that didn't need killing.

Hardin was the son of a Methodist preacher, and was even named for the founder of the Methodist sect. He learned the use of firearms at an early age. He was considered a good hunter and a marksman by the age of ten.

At fourteen years of age, (some accounts say twelve years) he stabbed a schoolmate. At 15 years of age, while visiting his uncle at Moscow, Texas, John and his cousin, Barnett Jones, challenged Mage, an ex-slave of his uncle's, to a wrestling match.

John Wesley Hardin

During the scuffling John scratched Mage's face quite badly, infuriating, the black man. The following day, Mage was waiting in the road when John rode by on his horse

"I'm gonna kill you!" Mage yelled, and came threatening John with a big stick.

John wouldn't run. He had a pistol and yelled at Mage, "Get back or I'll shoot!" The black man kept coming and John shot him three times in the chest. When Mage died a few days later, young John became a fugitive.

Hardin was having an extremely lucky streak playing cards in Towash, Texas, a fact that infuriated his opponent Jim Bradley, the big loser in the card game.

"You win another hand and I'll cut out your liver," roared Bradley. Unarmed, Hardin politely excused himself, went to his room, and strapped on two six-guns.

Later that night, Hardin stepped into the main street of Towash wearing his guns. Down the street was Jim Bradley, also wearing a gun. He was looking for Hardin.

Bradley pulled his gun and fired at Hardin, but missed. Hardin drew both pistols and fired them at the same time, one bullet striking Bradley in the head and the other in the chest.

Hardin had been practicing an unusual cross-draw. He had sewn two holsters into a vest so that the butts of his two six-guns pointed inward toward his chest. Hardin's draw was one sweeping movement where he crossed his arms, yanked the two six-guns and moved them in a lightning fast arch.

He had practiced the movement for hours and hours each day, figuring it was much faster than the traditional draw. Hardin's fight with Bradley was witnessed by dozens of people. The word soon spread that the young outlaw had the fastest guns in the West.

Hardin's scrapes became more frequent. He rode into Horn Hill, Texas, where a circus had come to town. He got into a fight with one of the circus men. They both drew their guns, but Hardin was faster. His shot killed the man.

A week later, while drinking in a bar, he met a saloon girl. While escorting her home, a man jumped him from a dark alleyway, demanding his money. Hardin threw his money on the ground. When the thief bent down to pick it up, Hardin fired a single bullet into his head.

He was arrested in Longview, Texas for a killing he swears he did not commit. Two state policemen tied him on a horse with no saddle and set out on the road to Waco. Hardin pulled out a hidden pistol, killed one of the lawmen, and made his escape. He later forced a blacksmith to remove his shackles.

In 1871, two Union soldiers named Green Parramore and John Lackey came looking for Hardin. While they were getting a bite to eat, Hardin walked into the room.

"I hear you two are looking for John Wesley Hardin. Do you know what he looks like?" he asked.

"No, sure don't," said Parramore. "We have never seen him, but we are looking for him and when we find him, we plan to arrest him."

"Well," said Hardin, "you see him now!" He drew both pistols and shot both of the soldiers. Parramore died, but Lackey, wounded badly, ran from the building and survived.

At one point, Hardin fell in love with Jane Bowen. He wanted to delay marriage until he could get a fresh start somewhere else. She talked him out of that, wanting to get married right away. They married in March 1872 when the bridegroom was not quite twenty years old.

Hardin had not been married long when he ran into trouble again. Hardin was quite adept at playing ten pins. He had beaten most of the locals at the game when Phil Sublett, a local gunman, challenged Hardin for five dollars a set. Hardin quickly beat Sublett six straight games.

The angry Sublett left the bar, but returned a few minutes later with a shotgun, shooting both barrels in

Hardin's direction. Although one load of buckshot caught Hardin in the side, he still managed to draw his six-guns, stagger into the street, and shoot the fleeing Sublett in the back.

When his first child, Molly was born, Hardin did make an attempt at rehabilitation. He rode into Gonzales, Texas, and surrendered his guns to Sheriff Richard Reagan, stating that would face all charges against him and wipe the slate clean.

When he learned that authorities were gathering evidence for as many killings as possible to pin on Hardin, the outlaw had second thoughts. A relative smuggled him a small saw, and he cut his way through a window and escaped.

When deputy sheriff Charles Webb rode into Comanche, Texas, Hardin's hometown, he was intent on arresting the outlaw. When Webb approached one of the saloons, Hardin appeared in front of him, spreading his coat backward to reveal his guns.

"Have you any papers for my arrest?" he asked Webb.

"I don't know you," Webb lied.

"My name is John Wesley Hardin," replied the gunfighter.

"Now I know you," said Webb, "but I have no papers for your arrest."

Hardin nodded, inviting Webb into the saloon for a drink. As Hardin turned to go through the swinging doors, someone yelled at Hardin, "Look out!"

With incredible speed, Hardin whirled about, cross-drawing his guns as he turned. Webb's gun had barely cleared its holster when Hardin fired, sending a bullet into the sheriff's head.

The State of Texas posted a four thousand dollar reward "dead or alive" for Hardin.

Hardin took the alias J.H. Swain. He packed up, taking his wife and baby to Florida where he hoped to start a new life. A baby boy was soon born, and the family then moved to Alabama.

He made a living by buying and selling horses, and later went into the logging business.

When his wife, homesick for her family, had written them, lawmen got on Hardin's tail again. They arrested him while he was aboard a train.

He stood trial in Gonzales, Texas. He defended himself in court.

"Gentlemen," Hardin told the court, "I swear before God that I never shot a man except in self-defense. Sheriff Webb came to Comanche for the purpose of arresting me, and I knew it.

"I met him and I defied him to arrest me, but I did not threaten him. I knew it was in his mind to kill me, not arrest me. Everybody knows he was a dangerous man with a pistol. I know I don't have any friends here but I don't blame them for being afraid to come out for me.

"My father was a good man, and my brother, who was lynched, never harmed a man in his life. People will call me a killer, but I swear to you gentlemen that I have shot only in defense of myself. And when Sheriff Webb drew his pistol, I had to draw mine. Anybody else would have done the same thing. Sheriff Webb had shot a lot of men. That's all, gentlemen."

Hardin walked back to the defendant's table and sat down. The jury found Hardin guilty of second-degree murder. He was sentenced to twenty-five years in prison at hard labor.

In prison, Hardin read anything he could. He read the Bible, books on religion, history, politics, mathematics, and science. He studied the dictionary. As the years passed, he developed into an educated man.

His wife Jane died while he was still in prison. She had faithfully written him every Sunday, and had operated a small farm to care for the children.

Harden was released from prison on February 17, 1894. He moved to El Paso where he studied law and stayed out of trouble. He also wrote an autobiography. Ironically, he was hailed in the El Paso Times as a living example of modern penal rehabilitation.

Yet, Hardin was the epitome of the western gun fighter. In terms of speed, accuracy, and ruthlessness, he was right at the top. Throughout his seven years of gun fighting, he is said to have killed at least forty-one men.

Hardin had killed at least a dozen men by the time he was seventeen. In one dramatic gunfight, he took on seven Mexicans along the Little Arkansas River, killing five of them.

On August 19, 1895, Hardin entered the Acme Saloon at the corner of San Antonio and Mesa streets in El Paso. He picked up the dice, rolled them down the bar, turned to a grocer, and said, "Brown, you have four sixes to beat."

At that instant, Constable John Selman stepped through the door, fired four quick shots, and Hardin was dead. Eyewitnesses say Hardin even drew while falling to the floor.

Chapter 13

Rattlesnake Dick

'The pirate of the placers'

"Rattlesnake Dick" was an honest gold miner. His moniker came not from being a sneaky character, but rather from the fact he settled in an area known as Rattlesnake Bar, near Auburn.

Dick Barter was born in Quebec City. When his parents died about 1850, Dick, his brother, and his cousin decided to head to the California gold strikes.

Towns in the area carried a wide array of unusual place names, such as Shirt Tail Canyon, Humbug Bar, Milk Punch Bar, Hell's Delight, and Ladies' Canyon.

Some of the best ore was being found on Rattlesnake Bar on the American River. All claims there were already staked, so Dick Barter, his cousin and his brother went to work for other miners.

After a year, his cousin and brother tired of the hard work of gold mining and returned home. Dick stayed on. He was confident there would be a new gold find. It was an old time miner, hearing of Dick's confidence in a new find that pinned his nickname on Barton. "Good for you, Rattlesnake Dick," said the miner.

About this time, a storeowner was missing some cattle. A person with a score to settle with Dick Barter accused him of being the thief. Barter was found innocent, but the stigma stuck. Later, a man working on the north fork had a mule stolen from him.

Dick Barter was convicted of theft on the flimsy evidence that he had been in that area. While Dick sweated in jail, the real thief confessed. Even though he was exonerated from both accusations, it always galled him.

Otherwise he might never have become an outlaw. He felt there was a smirch on his reputation around Rattlesnake Bar so Dick decided to change his name and move to the northern town of Shasta.

His move to Shasta, along with a name change, failed to give him the new start he wanted. A former neighbor from Rattlesnake Bar passed through Shasta and spotted Dick. He readily told the townsmen of Dick's suspect character.

"Well," Dick told himself, "if I'm going to be accused of being a thief, I might as well become one."

Dick quickly began the task of living up to his unsavory reputation. In his first outlaw episode, he pounced on a lone traveler, taking four hundred dollars, boasting to the victim as he left, "You have just been robbed by 'Rattlesnake Dick, the Pirate of the Placers'".

He followed that robbery with a number of others during 1856. He decided to form his own outlaw gang. He chose as his lieutenant George Skinner. The rest of the gang was Cyrus Skinner (George's brother), Big Dolph Newton, Romero, and Bill Carter.

Barter gave the gang some training by pulling a number of small jobs in Placer and Nevada counties in the Sierra Nevada foothills. This was practice for the big job that Dick had in mind.

Rattlesnake Dick's big goal was to rob a pack train taking gold out of Shasta and Trinity counties. His challenge was to figure out how to haul away the gold once they had gotten it. They opted to steal some mules to do this job.

The band easily got the drop on the pack train and escaped to their hideout. Dick and Cyrus Skinner rode off to get their stolen mules. Several days passed and Dick and Cyrus did not return. The rest of the men got nervous.

George Skinner had been left in charge. He decided to bury half the loot, and divide the other half among the four remaining men, making the load light enough to carry. They rode to a hideout they had near Auburn.

While there, a posse led by Wells Fargo detective Jack Barkeley caught them. George was killed in the gunfight. Romero was wounded. Newton and Carter both surrendered. They each got ten years at Angel Island. Carter got off, however, because he led Wells Fargo agents to the hideout where the gold was stashed.

The reason that Dick Barter and Cyrus Skinner had not returned was because they had been arrested in Placer County for the attempted theft of the mules. They escaped before their trial, but Cyrus was recaptured and sentenced to four years in the state prison.

With vengeance in his heart, Dick returned to Auburn country and assembled a new gang. He would show his accusers, who had ruined his name and reputation, what a bandit he could really be. For the next six years, Rattlesnake Dick plundered the roads from Nevada City to Folsom. For two years he got away with more robberies in five California counties.

Rattlesnake Dick didn't always get away with his escapades. He was often caught and thrown in the local jail to await trial. Just as often, he proved his slipperiness by escaping his jailers.

Newspaper accounts noted Rattlesnake Dick "broke out of every jail in Placer and Nevada counties". This was a little too much for the staid townsmen of Auburn, where peace and quiet was more desired than was the roughhousing of other gold towns.

Rattlesnake Dick became brazen in his approach to highway robbery. He and a companion boarded a stage in Nevada City that was apparently carrying a gold shipment. While the pair calmly took their seats, the news of their boarding reached Placer County's deputy sheriff.

"Enough is enough," thought the deputy. He would stop the stage at Harmon Hill and arrest the pair.

As the deputy halted the stage, the two bandits remained calm and unimpressed.

"Would the deputy mind just showing us a warrant for our arrest?" they asked.

As the deputy reached for the warrant, Rattlesnake Dick and his partner sent a barrage of bullets through the stagecoach windows. The deputy returned fire, using a one-shot derringer.

Before the deputy could reload, the bandits departed the stage, bidding the bewildered deputy goodbye, but not without imparting a few rude remarks about his abilities. No one was injured in the incident.

As his success as a bandit grew, so did Rattlesnake's boldness. In 1859, he and another outlaw companion rode openly through the streets of Auburn, a blatant affront to this serene little town. A three-man posse who was outraged by the effrontery of the outlaw pair accosted them. The two were ordered to halt by the posse leader.

"Who are you, and what do you want?" Dick demanded, at the same time drawing a weapon and firing.

One member of the posse was killed while the other two returned fire. A lawman's bullet hit Dick. He lurched in his saddle but managed to gallop off with his companion.

Dick's body was found along the roadside the next morning. It was carried back into town the next day by the Auburn stage.

But highway robbers just wouldn't leave the quiet town of Auburn alone. After Rattlesnake Dick's demise, highwayman Tom Bell became Auburn's nemesis.

Bell was said to be a doctor by profession, a calling at which he apparently failed. Neither did he make it as a miner or as a gambler. Failing at all else, he turned to armed robbery.

He hid out in at least three highway taverns, whose owners tipped him off on the departures of their well-heeled guests. The raids of Bell and his gang became such an outrage that lawmen in all of northern California determined to stop the lawbreakers.

When Placer County's sheriff caught up with the gang at one point, Bell slipped away, hiding out near Firebaugh's Ferry on the San Joaquin River. There, a posse surprised him. Taken without a fight, Bell was hung without fanfare.

This allowed Auburn to resume its former quiet and unexciting community life.

Chapter 14

Clay Allison

Clay Allison was obviously a mental case, a fact that his medical discharge from the Tennessee Light Artillery attests to. Allison wanted to fight for the Confederacy, but his mentality came into question after a brief time in the artillery.

Allison had a clubfoot, but that did not seem to hamper his ability to perform active duty, but his mental condition apparently did. His medical discharge noted: "Incapable of performing the duties of a soldier because of a blow received many years ago. Emotional or physical excitement produces paroxysmals of a mixed character, partly epileptic and partly maniacal."

Clay Allison with cast on leg.

He once had threatened to kill his commanders because they would not pursue Union troops that were running away from the fight.

Clay returned home to his parent's farm following his discharge. One day, a corporal with the Third Illinois Cavalry rode onto the farm boasting that he was going to take everything he could get his hands on from the family home. Allison secured a gun from a closet and killed the soldier.

Once the war was officially over, Allison and his brothers, Monroe and John, and their sister Mary and her husband, Lewis Coleman, headed to the Brazos River country in Texas.

He accused Zachary Colbert, a ferryman, of overcharging the group to cross the river. Clay attacked him, leaving him unconscious. The Allisons then rode across the Red River into Texas...free of charge.

In Texas, Allison worked as a trail boss for Oliver Loving and Charles Goodnight, two legendary Texas cattlemen. He also worked for two other noted cattlemen, M.L. Dalton and Isaac Lacy. All Allison asked in payment for his riding chores was three hundred head of cattle, enough to start his own ranch near the town of Cimarron in Colfax County, New Mexico Territory.

His fiery temper flared when the wife of Charles Kennedy in Elizabethtown, New Mexico, told Clay her husband had gone on a rampage. He first killed some strangers, she said, and when he arrived home, he killed their own daughter.

Allison gathered some of his drinking companions to go after Kennedy. They brought him to the Elizabethtown jail. Then, bones were found at the Kennedy ranch, though they had not been determined to be human bones.

The hot-tempered Allison and his companions again exploded into the Elizabethtown jail, and hauled Kennedy kicking and screaming to the local slaughterhouse. Not only was Kennedy lynched, but Allison decapitated the body, and displayed the head on a pole at Lambert's

Saloon. In his own way, Allison considered that justice had been served.

An enemy of Allison's came riding into Cimarron, looking for a fight. Chunk Colbert wanted revenge for his uncle who was the ferryman that wanted to overcharge the Allison group to cross the river.

Colbert was already credited with killing seven men, and he wanted to make Clay Allison his eighth. Colbert challenged Allison to a horse race. The race ended in a draw.

The men, while wary of each other, decided to dine together at the Clifton House. Clay laid his pistol conspicuously on the table next to his plate. Colbert laid his across his lap at full cock.

After a few bites, Clay noticed Chunk reach for a cup of coffee with one hand and his pistol with the other. Allison tipped his chair backward, falling toward the floor, which caused Colbert to hurry his shot and miss. Clay killed him with a shot squarely in the head.

He was asked why he would sit down to eat with a man who intended to kill him.

"Because I didn't want to send a man to hell on an empty stomach," he replied.

Allison's behavior became even more bizarre. He was reported to have stripped to nothing but his hat, boots and guns while in Canadian, Texas, looking for a fight with somebody, anybody. Nobody obliged him.

Another time, he rode totally naked on his horse up and down the streets of the town, whooping and hollering, declaring drinks were on him at the local saloon.

The compulsive gunman then got involved in a lynching. A Mexican named Cruz Vega was charged with murder. Allison took Vega bodily from the jail. As Vega

119

screamed his innocence, he was hanged from a telegraph pole. Clay then shot the man in the back to, as he said, "to put the poor Mex out of his misery."

He then tied the Mexican's body behind his horse and galloped through the streets of the town and into the rough terrain outside of town. When he had finished, Vega was unrecognizable. Allison then cut Vega's body from his horse, and left it for the buzzards in the desert.

The citizens of Colfax County were tired of the escapades of Clay Allison. They wanted to get him out of the county. Even Lewis Coleman, Clay's brother in law, wanted him gone.

Allison did have a staunch companion in his brother John, however. One evening, after Clay and John had returned off the trail from selling cattle, they spotted a local social taking place. They crashed the party, dancing with several unwilling partners.

Deputy Charles Faber arrived, and asked the Allison brothers to remove their weapons, an order which went unheard. Faber deputized two men, then with shotgun in hand, led them back into the social.

As the lawmen came through the door, someone warned, "Look out!" As John Allison went for his gun, Faber shot him. Clay, who was at the bar, spun around and fired four shots at Faber, one of which was fatal.

Allison then dragged the body of Faber over to his wounded brother. "Look here, this man is dead, John. Not to worry, vengeance is ours! Not to worry!" John Allison did recover.

People in Colfax County refused to do any more business with Clay Allison. He moved to Hemphill County, Texas, got married, and had a daughter. He still preferred New Mexico.

He bought a ranch in Lincoln County and did well for a time.

His maniacal actions continued again in Cheyenne, Wyoming. Allison, on a long, hard cattle drive, had a toothache. He went to a local dentist. The dentist, who was well aware of Allison's reputation, worked on the wrong tooth.

Allison left, going to another dentist who did the job correctly. Irritated, Allison went back to the first dentist and was holding the man down, doing his best to extract every tooth in the dentist's head. The dentist's screams brought men in to pull the angry Allison off the petrified man.

When Clay was returning from Pecos, Texas, with a wagon full of supplies, a sack of grain is believed to have fallen. As he grabbed for it, Allison fell from the wagon and underneath one of the wheels. Some say he had been drinking. The horses reared and lunged forward. The heavy buckboard crushed Alison's neck and nearly decapitated him

Historians estimate that the six-foot, blue-eyed gunman shot and killed at least fifteen men. Shortly before his death, he told a newsman, "I never killed a man who didn't need it."

Chapter 15

Big Bob Brady

While Big Bob Brady was just as notorious, he never reached the legendary status of other desperados such as "Pretty Boy" Floyd, "Machine Gun" Kelly, Clyde Barrow, Harvey Bailey, and Wilbur Underhill.

His criminal career began at age fifteen. He was charged with grand larceny and sent to State Industrial Reformatory at Hutchinson, Kansas for a five-year sentence.

Brady was in and out of prisons frequently, mostly on petty thefts, forgery, and other crimes.

But on September 15, 1931, he and Clarence "Buck" Adams indulged in a more serious matter. They robbed the First National Bank at Texhoma, Oklahoma of fifty three hundred dollars.

His old nemesis, Sheriff O.L. Clark, tracked Brady and Adams to the Carlsbad Caverns in New Mexico. The pair was returned to Guymon for trial. Brady then attempted a jailbreak.

During a scuffle with a deputy, Brady was shot. The bullet entered his head just below the left eye, passed through his skull, narrowly missing his brain, and exited below his left ear.

Rushed to Epworth Hospital at Liberal, Kansas, Brady recovered, but had to wear glasses and could never completely close his left eyelid again. Jokesters quipped the law would have a tougher time catching Brady now, as he "slept with one eye open."

Later, Brady was convicted of robbery with firearms. He was returned to McAlister prison under a thirty-five year sentence.

He was assigned to the prison overalls shop and devised a unique escape. Aided by fellow prisoners, he crawled inside an overalls crate in a shipment due to leave the prison.

Inmates deliberately loaded the crate containing Brady at the rear of the truck. When the truck was a safe distance from prison, Brady pushed up the lid, climbed out of the crate, and jumped from the truck.

Brady's escapades following that escape are somewhat blurry and difficult to follow. What is known is that farmer Henry Kohlenberg and his son Lloyd, spotted four suspicious men crossing their pasture, armed with shotguns.

Big Bob Brady was a part of the group. Under sheriff Harve R. Lininger and Deputy Ed Schlotman at first believed the men were rabbit hunters, but decided to question them anyway. Lininger asked Brady, who was in front of the group, for his name.

"That's all right what my name is, Buddy," snarled Brady. He then leveled his shotgun at Deputy Lininger and pulled the trigger. The gun misfired and both Deputies Lininger and Schlotman returned the fire.

Brady, failing at reloading his weapon, attempted to run away. Schlotman grabbed a shotgun from his car, fired on Brady, and the outlaw dropped to his knees. He then stood up, ran about thirty yards, collapsed and died. His wife, Leona Brady, arrived in Ada, Oklahoma to make funeral arrangements. She is said to have expressed regrets "that Brady hadn't killed fifty officers before he got shot."

Chapter 16

Bonnie and Clyde

This duo was considered two of the most notorious desperados during the Depression years of the 1930s. Clyde Barrow and Bonnie Parker slaughtered at least a dozen men, most of who were peace officers.

Still, in retrospect, they were penny-ante bandits. Bonnie and Clyde were never known for their expertise at big bank robberies. They were better known for their bungled robberies of grocery stores and gas stations.

Both were born into poverty. Clyde Chestnut Barrow was raised in the slums of West Dallas, the son of a former sharecropper.

Bonnie married young, too young. Less than a year after her marriage her scatterbrained husband, Roy Thornton, was sentenced to ninety-nine years At Huntsville as a habitual criminal.

Early on, Clyde was sentenced to two years in prison for two burglaries and five car thefts. Several other minor thefts and jail breaks followed during his early career. He then hooked up with Bonnie Parker Thornton.

The pair wrecked their car in a railway culvert, and then fled on foot to another road. They flagged down a motorist and took his car at gunpoint. Then only fifteen miles later, they lost a wheel from the stolen car. Stealing still another vehicle from a farmer, they escaped.

During the time, breadlines and soup kitchens adorned every city. Both Bonnie and Clyde abhorred poverty.

Clyde picked up Bonnie in Dallas. Clyde's brother Buck, freshly out of prison, and his wife, Blanche, then joined the pair. This was the real start of the Barrow Gang.

The foursome terrorized banks and storeowners in five states---Texas, Oklahoma, Missouri, Louisiana, and New Mexico. Their escapades seemed to thrill destitute Americans. One historian, Jonathan Davis, said, "Anybody who robbed banks or fought the law were really living out some secret fantasies on a large part of the public."

Clyde was arrested February 12, 1930 and taken to Waco County Courthouse for trial. During one of her visitations with Clyde, Bonnie met Frank Turner, a two-time loser.

He convinced Bonnie to go to his parent's home and get a gun they had, and to smuggle it into the jail where she would give it to Clyde. The two, Turner explained, would then escape. Bonnie gladly followed his directions.

Clyde and Turner subdued their guard as he slid a food tray under their cell. He locked the jailor in the cell and Clyde and Turner walked out.

Rather than returning to Dallas where police would naturally be waiting, Clyde and Turner went to Illinois, performing such petty robberies as service stations, fruit stands and small grocery markets.

Clyde had learned a tactic to keep police off his trail. He stole license plates frequently and changed them after each robbery. A delay in changing a plate after one holdup resulted in him being recaptured. A passerby had memorized his license and reported it to police, who caught him soon thereafter.

Clyde was taken back to Waco County, and sentenced to 14-years in the dreaded Eastham Prison Farm Number 2 in Huntsville, which one author referred to as an inferno on the Texas plains.

Author John Neal Phillips, in his book, Running with Bonnie and Clyde, noted that guards would draw straws to see who among them would have the pleasure of beating such and such prisoner.

So that he could receive letters from her, Clyde had listed Bonnie as his wife on official status papers. Prisoners were only allowed correspondence from blood family members or a spouse.

Clyde then convinced a fellow prisoner to cut off two of his toes to avoid hard labor. The so-called accident also led to his early release from prison, walking on crutches.

He picked Bonnie up in Dallas. They were constantly on the run, robbing small food stores and service stations as they went.

One time, near Springtown, Oklahoma, Bonnie and Clyde and Raymond Hamilton saw a country-dance taking place in Stringtown, Oklahoma. Sheriff C. G. Maxwell and Deputy Eugene Moore approached them on the dance floor. They had noticed Hamilton taking a swig of something as he emerged from the car.

Both Clyde and Hamilton responded with gunfire, killing Deputy Moore outright and seriously wounding Sheriff Maxwell. They roared off, with townspeople in pursuit.

Bonnie Parker was severely burned in a car accident on the Salt Fork of the Red River. She and Clyde holed up at the Dennis Tourist Court on U.S. Hiway 64 in Fort Smith, Arkansas.

Clyde Barrow was still staying at the Dennis Tourist Court when the Commercial Bank in nearby Alma, Arkansas was robbed of several thousand dollars. During that robbery, town marshal H.D. Humphrey was captured by the bandits and tied to a column with wire.

After one robbery of a "Piggly Wiggly" market in Fayetteville, Arkansas, where they netted a pitiful thirty-five dollars, the robbers fled in the owner's truck, which was found, abandoned a few blocks away.

The pair's next fiasco occurred when the stolen vehicle they were driving rammed the rear end of a car driven by automobile dealer Webber Wilson. Marshal Humphrey, whom they had tied up in the Alma bank robbery, had been pursuing the pair and witnessed the crash.

When Humphrey approached their car, both machine gun and shotgun fire erupted from the car. Humphrey fell to the ground. Before he died in a hospital, Humphrey identified one occupant of the car as Clyde Barrow.

Quickly grabbing weapons from their wrecked car, the gang commandeered another car, returned to the Dennis Tourist Court in Fort Smith, packed their goods, and quickly left Arkansas.

A short time later, the Barrow Gang shot it out with lawmen near Dexter, Iowa. Buck Barrow, Clyde's brother, was fatally wounded and lawmen recovered the .38 Smith and Wesson pistol that had been stolen from marshal Humphrey.

Clyde Barrow was always having car trouble. In one episode, Clyde and Bonnie's blue Ford sedan was parked just off Hiway 114 near Grapevine, Texas. Highway Patrolmen, H.D. Murphy and E.B. Wheeler, decided to investigate the vehicle.

They had no sooner racked their motorcycles than shots rang out, claiming the lives of both lawmen.

Word was sent out to lawmen that Barrow might be wearing a steel vest. On April 6, 1934, Barrow's muddy Ford was parked just off Hiway 66 near Commerce, Oklahoma. Bonnie, Clyde, and an escaped convict, Henry Methvin were taking a much-need rest.

A local resident passed the scene and thought the occupants of the car might be in trouble. He reported the situation to Constable Cal Campbell of Commerce.

When Campbell and Police Chief Percy Boyd went to investigate, parking their car in front of the Ford. Clyde Barrow, seeing the officers, started his vehicle, shifted into reverse, and began backing down the road. The unlucky Barrow backed into a drainage ditch.

Barrow jumped from the car with a Browning automatic rifle. He fired two 20 round clips at the officers. Officer Campbell was struck down, and Officer Boyd was knocked unconscious by a bullet to the head.

When Boyd gained consciousness, convict Methvin was standing over him with a metal bar.

"Get up and come with me," he told the wounded officer. "We're going to take you with us."

Barrow, in the meantime, had gone to a nearby house to get a car. He drove it up to the Ford, and attempted to pull it from the ditch with a towrope. The rope broke.

As others arrived on the scene where Constable Campbell lay dead in the road, Barrow and Methvin stood in the road with guns drawn and ordered people to push the Ford to get it unstuck. It remained mired in the ditch.

Finally, Charley Dodson arrived in a truck. Barrow ordered Dodson to back up to the muddy Ford automobile and pull it from the mud. When the car was free, Barrow then ordered Methvin and Officer Boyd to get into the back seat.

Barrow turned the vehicle around in the middle of the road and headed across the Neosha River Bridge. They let Officer Boyd out at a place called Mangel Corner, near Fort Scott, Kansas.

Boyd asked Bonnie what he should tell the world when he got back. She said, "Tell them I don't smoke cigars!"

Bonnie and Clyde were slain in an ambush near Sailes, Louisiana, on May 23, 1934. Six officers had ambushed the two notorious killers.

Chapter 17

Ma Barker

Was Ma Barker the clever mastermind behind the crimes committed by the Barker-Karpis Gang? Or was she an ignorant hillbilly mother who only wanted to defend her sons?

One thing is certain; Ma Barker knew her sons were criminals. She willingly joined them in moving from one place to another to avoid the police and to act as cover.

According to one member of the gang, Harvey Bailey, Ma Barker wasn't much of a thinker. "The old woman couldn't plan breakfast," he told author L.L. Edge. Alvin Karpis himself characterized Ma Barker as an ignorant old hillbilly woman who traveled about with her sons, who used her as a cover.

The Barker brothers included Herman, Lloyd, Fred and Arthur. Their mother was Arizona Barker, commonly known as Kate or "Arrie" Barker. According to an F.B.I. file, the sons of Ma Barker were essentially illiterate.

The F.B.I. notes that Kate Barker separated from her husband George Barker sometime in 1928. It was about this time that sons Herman, Lloyd and Arthur Barker all received prison sentences, according to F.B.I. notes, "It is possible that Kate became loose in her moral life at that time."

Kate Barker, the F.B.I. maintains, dominated her sons "with an iron will". Fred and Arthur, especially, were submissive to her.

Ma Barker liked to live well. She purchased expensive clothing, furniture and other necessities from the spoils of her sons' activities. "Ma Barker was also very jealous of her boys and did not wish to have them associated with girl friends," F.B.I. notes claim.

Gang member Harvey Bailey disputed her intelligence. "When we'd sit down to plan a bank job," he said, "she'd go into the other room and listen to Amos and Andy or hillbilly music on the radio."

J. Edgar Hoover characterized Ma Barker as "a monument to the evils of parental indulgence." Ma Barker's troubles seem rooted in her blind devotion to her sons. Her actions, essentially, were the same as the doting mothers of the James's, the Youngers, the Daltons, and the Barrows.

Ma Barker, according to the F.B.I files, boasted to her neighbors, "I got great days ahead of me, when my children grow up. Silk dresses, fur coats and diamond rings."

Some feel the F.B.I. did all it could to propagate the myth of a "Bloody Mama" character, rather than that of a protective mother.

Some reports claim that when neighbors complained about the pranks and destructive activity of the Barker boys in their younger years, their father, George Barker, would shrug and say, "You'll have to talk to Mother. She handles the boys."

While Fred Barker was in the Kansas State Penitentiary, he formed a friendship with Alvin Karpis. Karpis was assigned to work the coalmines at the prison. Karpis arranged with other prisoners to buy their "pay coal" in order to hasten his release.

Prisoners were required to dig a certain quantity of coal each day. Each ton mined over the required amount, the prisoner was given "good time". Karpis was released from prison on May 31, 1951 because of the pay coal he purchased.

Following their release, Fred Barker and Karpis committed several small-time robberies. They used a 1951 Desoto automobile in a store robbery. They then drove into the Davidson Motor Company garage in West Plains, Missouri for some repair work.

The repairman recognized the car as the one used in the store robbery the previous day. He notified sheriff C.E. Kelly, who came to investigate. Barker and Karpis fired on Sheriff Kelly, killing him.

Both Herman and Lloyd Barker were out of the picture in the early 30s when Ma Barker's gang began their violent Midwest crime spree. Herman had been killed in a shootout with police in Wichita.

Freddy and Arthur (better known as Dock) made up for the absence of the brothers. They were bloodthirsty and money hungry at the same time.

Freddy and Arthur teamed up with Alvin "Creepy" Karpis. Using Ma Barker as their cover, they were responsible for dozens of bank robberies, kidnappings and murders, including the abductions of William Hamm, Jr. of the Hamm Beer Empire, and banker Edward Bremer.

Ma Barker had taken on a lover, a drunken sign painter by the name of George W. Dunlop. Dunlop drove the boys crazy with his lazy, drunken, loose tongue ways. The boys thought it was Dunlop who once tipped the cops off to their location.

After clearing it with Ma Barker, the boys killed Dunlop, leaving his body on the shore of a Wisconsin lake.

Federal agents finally caught up with Dock in Chicago in 1934. They arrested him while he was taking a walk, without a gun. When the agents rummaged through Dock's apartment, they found a map of Florida.

Circled on the map was the tiny resort town of Ocklawaha. The federal agents, following the lead, found Fred and Ma holed up in a cabin at the resort.

A four-hour gun battle ensued, and 1500 rounds of ammunition were poured into the house. Eventually, the feds pushed themselves inside the cabin. Fred's body was riddled with bullets, and Ma Barker had a single bullet-hole in her forehead. She was clutching a Thompson sub-machine gun.

Dock, put on trial for the kidnapping of the Hamm's beer magnate, was sentenced to Alcatraz. He served 10 years, and then decided to try an escape. Prison guards shot him on the island's shore.

Pa Barker received all of the bodies back at his mountain home in Missouri. He buried them in the back.

For years, it is said that curious visitors would stop and Barker would point out the graves of his beloved sweet family.

Chapter 18

Wilbur Underhill

Wilber Underhill was sort of a two-bit bandit, even after escaping from the state prison at McAlester, Oklahoma. He took his 19-year-old nephew, who admired his uncle, along with him.

The pair's first holdup was the Fox-Midland Theater in Coffeyville, Kansas. Oddly, the holdup, which yielded about three hundred dollars, was on "bank night". An arrest warrant quickly followed.

In his second robbery, a Texaco gasoline station, he collected a measly fourteen-dollars-and-sixty-eight-cents.

The pair headed to Wichita to let things cool down. They rented a room at the Iris Hotel. About eight o'clock in the morning, there was a knock on their door. Police officer Merle Colver was checking on all strangers at the hotel.

He spotted photographs on a table that would have sent Underhill back to prison. Underhill drew a pistol from under a pillow and fired into Colver's back while he was inspecting the evidence. As Colver turned, another shot went into the lawman's head.

Wilber's shirt had Colver's blood on it. He ripped off and threw away the bloodied shirt. Later, he realized the keys to the car he had parked at the Lucas Garage were in the shirt.

The outlaw, then shirtless, acquired a coat with which he covered his face by turning up the collar. This brought even more attention to him because it was a hot summer day. He had also left the photos that had so interested police officer Colver at the crime scene.

Later, two police officers saw Underhill and his nephew slinking along, Wilber carrying the heavy coat he had stolen over his arm. When officer Jack Myler shouted at the two men to stop. Wilber pulled a pistol from the coat's pocket. Officer Myler fired a shot, hitting Underhill in the arm.

Wilber surrendered. Frank Underhill was also apprehended. The pair were taken to police headquarters and confessed to killing Officer Colver.

"Officer Colver didn't do as I requested," he told his questioners.

He was no sooner ensconced in Kansas State Penitentiary than he started planning an escape. Soon, he teamed up with several other prisoners to make a break.

When one prisoner said he would like to make the prison break without hurting any prison officials, Underhill snarled, "Don't be like that. I wouldn't miss a chance to kill a bunch of lousy 'screws'. And if I'm going to be in this break, I'm going to knock a few punks over, just to be doing."

One of the prisoners weakened before the escape, and informed the warden of the proposed prison break. Underhill was put into solitary confinement. His next attempt at escape succeeded.

Underhill was involved in a string of bank robberies in 1933. Many of these robberies included Harvey Bailey, who had joined Underhill in his last escape from prison.

"He always wanted to kill someone," Bailey said. "We'd drive through some town and every time he saw a cop he wanted to kill him. He would buy gasoline and get mad and want to kill the man instead of paying him."

Two bandits walked into the Purity Drug Store in Okmulgee, Oklahoma just before closing time. It was near midnight on Christmas Day. They demanded of Ira B. Maynard, the store's owner, "Give us that sack of money you just got done fixing up."

Mrs. Maynard, taking advantage of the darkness in the store, had put the money sack between her knees. Mr. Maynard told the bandits, "The only money we have is in the till."

The inept bandits then dropped the till as they pulled it from the cash register. One of the bandits began scooping up the fallen cash, and had collected about twenty-five dollars when young George Fee and C.B. Kerr both walked into the store.

The taller of the bandits shoved a single-action pistol in their faces and commanded, "Raise your hands!" The nineteen-year-old Fee moved toward the bandits.

The shorter of the bandits fired a bullet into Fee's chest. When Fee dropped to the floor, the bandits fled. An ambulance took Fee to the hospital, but he died with his mother at his bedside.

Police were unable to gather an accurate description of the bandits due mainly to the poor lighting in the store. A few days later, Wilber Underhill and Ike Akins were arrested and connected to the robbery.

F.B.I. agents got word that Underhill was staying at 606 West Dewey Street in Shawnee, Oklahoma, with his recent bride, Hazel Hudson.

Detective Clarence O. Hurt gave a detailed account to the press.

"We rode out of Oklahoma City about midnight after we got the tip that Underhill was at Shawnee. We got together at the police station there and sent a car out to scout the house.

"They came back and said Underhill was still up and there was drinking going on. We waited, and planned how every man would station himself so we wouldn't be shooting each other and into the house next door.

"The back of the house is to the north, and there is a bedroom on the northeast corner. We figured that was where Underhill and his wife would be."

Hurt and one other agent sneaked up to the bedroom window. A dog in the neighborhood started barking.

"We looked in and Underhill was at the foot of his bed in his underwear, heading toward us, as though he wanted to see why that dog was barking.

"This is the law, Wilber, stick'em up," Hurt yelled.

"Okay," he replied, raising his hands about halfway to his head.

He then whirled and grabbed two Lugers off a little table by the bed.

"All three of us fired at once," Hurt said. "I hit him with a gas bullet at the same instant Agent Colvin's machine gun started rolling. Underhill's guns were also spurting fire."

Underhill dashed out the front door. He was found downtown several hours later, bleeding from several bullet holes.

"It all happened in less than two minutes," said Hurt, "and I'd say 200 shots were fired. Underhill fired 60 of them."

The outlaw was sent to a prison hospital. He died there on January 6, 1934.

Oklahoma had only a $100 reward for the delivery of Wilber Underhill, while Kansas offered a $500 reward. Both were considered pitifully small as Underhill was considered one of the most dangerous outlaws around.

Chapter 19

Machine Gun Kelly

Some regarded George "Machine Gun" Kelly as a criminal buffoon who blustered his way onto the nation's public enemy roster. At the same time, the FBI says, it was "Machine Gun" Kelly that gave federal agents their colorful nickname of "G-Men".

One account says that as a teenager, George learned that his father was having an affair. He confronted him, demanding a higher weekly allowance and use of the family's automobile. His father agreed.

George became involved in bootlegging while still in high school. Tennessee had begun state prohibition and George now had use of an automobile, thanks to his father's extramarital romance.

He was arrested in Memphis for possession of alcohol He called his father to bail him out. When George's mother died, his relationship with his father deteriorated badly.

Years later, when George's first marriage was falling apart, he reportedly called his father.

"I'm committing suicide. Will you bury me Dad?" he asked.

"Gladly, son," came the reply.

The outlaw's real name was George Kelly Barnes, born in Memphis, Tennessee, July 18, 1895. He was briefly enrolled as a college student at Mississippi A&M to study agriculture. His college career was brief, as he had thirty-one demerits in the first semester and twenty-four more in the first few weeks of the second.

He tried cab driving for a while, but then decided there was more money to be made in "bootlegging". To protect his family name of Barnes, he adopted the alias of George R. Kelly. He expanded his bootlegging business in Texas, Oklahoma, Tennessee and Mississippi.

While imprisoned in Alcatraz, he once told Warden James A. Johnston, "My family are good people. Only I turned out to be a heel."

While drifting around Oklahoma, Kelly went to work for bootlegger "Little Steve" Anderson. Soon, a romance between George and Anderson's mistress, Kathryn Thorne developed.

Some say it is Kathryn that created "Machine Gun" Kelly. She supposedly bought Kelly his first Thompson sub-machine gun and made him practice with it.

Kathryn's third marriage was to a bootlegger named Charlie Thorne. When she later learned he was cheating on her she stopped at a gas station and told the attendant, "I'm bound for Coleman, Texas, to kill that God-damned Charlie Thorne."

He was found shot to death the next day. The coroner's report said it was suicide.

FBI records indicate that Kathryn once worked as a manicurist in Fort Worth. A local businessman asked her out on a date.

He later told a friend, "Remember that innocent little girl I was going to show a good time? She took me to more speakeasies, more bootleg dives, and more holes-in-the-wall than I thought existed in all of Texas."

George Kelly was caught smuggling whiskey onto an Indian Reservation and sentenced to three years in

Leavenworth. It is there that he made his first contacts with the big-time underworld.

During his short crime-filled career, he associated with such notorious gangsters as John Dillinger, "Pretty Boy" Floyd, "Baby Face" Nelson, Alvin "Creepy" Karpis, Bonnie and Clyde, and Ma Barker and the Barker Gang.

From 1931 to 1934, George "Machine Gun" Kelly participated in quite a number of bank robberies, one netting him seventy-seven thousand dollars.

Kelly's son, Bruce Barnes, who penned a biography of his dad, claimed that Kelly "felt superior" to the bank robbers he befriended, but also recognized their accomplishments.

Kidnapping soon became an integral part of Kelly's operations. One kidnapping included that of Charles F. Urschel, a millionaire oilman in Oklahoma City. It is also the one that put him away for life. Kelly, holding his customary machine gun, and his partner, Albert Bates entered the Urschel home where two couples were playing bridge.

When asked which man at the table was Urschel, neither spoke. Kelly and Bates loaded both of them into an automobile and took off. Outside the city, they did a quick search of the men's wallets, which revealed the true Charles Urschel.

After relieving Urschel's bridge playing partner, Walter Jarrett, of fifty-one dollars, he was deposited on the road. The outlaws retained Urschel for nine days, releasing him after getting two hundred thousand dollars in ransom money.

With the information that Urschel supplied, the FBI was able to pinpoint the Shannon Ranch where he had been held.

There are different accounts about "Machine Gun" Kelly's capture and arrest. One account is that Sergeant William Raney, of the Memphis Police Department, knocked on the door of a house where Kelly was known to be staying.

He found Kelly standing in his pajamas holding a .45. He had a hangover. The sergeant jammed his shotgun into Kelly's stomach and ordered him to drop the gun.

Kelly did, on his own foot.

The outlaw then muttered, "I've been waiting for you all night."

Following a trial, where a jury sentenced him to life in prison for Urschel's kidnapping, Kelly was sent to Leavenworth Penitentiary. Later, he was transferred to Alcatraz, in California's San Francisco Bay.

In 1951, George "Machine Gun" Kelly was transferred back to Leavenworth. He was assigned to the prison's furniture factory. He died of a massive heart attack on July 17, 1954. He was 54 years of age.

Chapter 20

Sam Bass

Sam Bass, as did most western outlaws, lived a short life. His start in life didn't help matters.

When he was ten years old, his mother died. Three years later his father died. Sam was sent to live with his uncle, a tight-lipped skinflint who denied his nephew any type of education.

Sam Bass

Sam was forced to work on his Uncle David Sheek's farm from morning until night. Things weren't much better after he ran away from his uncle's farm.

Bass built a raft when he was eight years old and floated down the Mississippi to St. Louis. From there, he drifted to Rosedale, Mississippi, where he worked as a mill hand, and as a teamster.

He teamed up with Joel Collins, a hell-raiser. They teamed up to drive a herd of cattle to Dodge City for their owners. Reaching Dodge City, they decided to drive the herd further north where prices were higher.

After selling the herd, Bass and Collins had eight thousand dollars in their pockets. Instead of returning to

Texas and paying the owners for the cattle, Bass and Collins gambled in Ogallala, Nebraska, and in the town of Deadwood, South Dakota. They lost the eight thousand dollars.

The pair then tried their hand at freighting, without success. The two uneducated men then decided to really make it big.

They formed a gang, consisting of Tom Nixon, Bill Heffridge, Jim Berry, Jack Davis, and Robert "Little Reddy" McKimie. On stolen horses, they held up the Deadwood Stage seven times, but none of the robberies yielded much. McKimie was kicked out of the gang after the first robbery because he killed the driver of the stage.

Jack Davis, a California bandit, suggested the gang attack the Union Pacific, noting that these trains carried huge gold shipments from the West.

Collins perfected a plan to rob the Union Pacific train at Big Springs, Nebraska. They got away with sixty thousand dollars in newly minted $20 gold pieces from the mail car, which were being shipped from the Denver Mint. Both Berry and Nixon then went to Missouri, where Berry was later killed. Nixon fled to Canada and was never heard from again.

Collins and Potts were both shot to death in an ambush at Buffalo Station, Kansas. Lawmen recovered twenty five thousand in gold pieces from Collins' saddlebags. Davis went to New Orleans, and Bass, disguised as a farmer, returned back to Texas, where he formed a new outlaw gang.

There, the gang held up two stagecoaches and robbed four trains within twenty-five miles of Dallas. The robberies yielded little in money, but they served to rouse up the citizens. A special company of Texas Rangers was assigned the task of hunting them down.

Bass and his gang eluded lawmen until one of the gang members, Jim Murphy, turned informer. Murphy, along with his father William Murphy, had been charged with harboring the Bass Gang and faced possible imprisonment. Murphy cut a deal with lawmen to save himself and his father.

Bass and his gang rode south to rob the Williamson County Bank in Round Rock, Texas. Murphy had clued the lawmen of the gang's intent.

When they entered town, the outlaws stopped at a tobacco store. Jim Murphy had told Bass he wanted to look around and make sure things were safe.

Sheriff Hoke Grimes and his deputy Maurice Moore watched the other three gang members. All were wearing long coats with suspicious bulges. Wearing concealed weapons was against a local ordinance. Grimes commented to his deputy, "I think one of those men has a six-shooter on."

Grimes stepped up behind Seaborn Barnes and, putting a friendly hand on his shoulder, ask if he was armed. Barnes yanked his coat open and drew his six-shooter, firing two bullets into the startled sheriff.

Before the sheriff had even hit the floor, Bass and Jackson shot him four more times, and sent two more bullets into the stomach of Deputy Moore.

Deputy Moore shot bass in the hand before he collapsed. While Bass struggled, Frank Jackson who was unhurt, helped Bass get on his horse. As the pair fled, Ranger Dick Ware shot Bass in the back.

Jackson stayed with Bass until the got out of town, at which point Bass, who was bleeding heavily, asked Jackson to stop.

Bass said, "Go on, Frank. I'm finished but you get going before the law gets here." He told Jackson to take all the gold in his saddlebags. Jackson complied and rode away. He was never heard from again.

Texas Rangers found Bass the following day, sitting under a tree where Jackson had left him. They brought Sam back to Round Rock, but he died the following day. It was his twenty-seventh birthday.

Chapter 21

Henry Starr

Henry Starr claimed he robbed more banks than both the James-Younger Gang and the Doolin-Dalton Gang put together. Yet, he said he killed only one man, a U.S. deputy marshal intent on arresting him.

Henry Starr

Starr began his outlaw career when bank robbers were still riding horseback, using a Colt .45 and a Winchester rifle. He ended it with the use of automobiles and automatic pistols. Starr's outlaw career spanned some 30 years, unusually long for any criminal.

Starr was born in Indian Territory where little or no law enforcement took place. The rugged region from which Starr came was often referred to as "Robbers Roost" where murderers, and criminals of all stripes could find refuge from pursuing lawmen.

The Starr family boasted of a number of outlaws. Henry's grandfather was Tom Starr, a man known as a fighter and an outlaw. His aunt was Belle Starr, whose

149

criminal escapades has been the subject of both books and movies.

Henry is said to have poor image of his aunt, Belle Starr. To him, she was crude. He was quick to inform people that she was his aunt only by marriage.

In 1893, Henry Starr was getting a reputation as a badman in Indian Territory. He was still searching for a bank he could rob that would put him in the big money.

His first confrontation with the law was for allegedly stealing another man's horse. Starr claimed the horse had simply wandered onto the ranch where he was working and he kept and cared for the animal for about a month. He was nevertheless arrested and sent to federal jail in Fort Smith. He was released shortly, but the event left him callous and with little regard for the law.

It was then he decided if he was going to be looked upon as an outlaw, he might as well be a good one.

He soon fell in with two known bandits, Ed Newcome and Jesse Jackson, both on the law's wanted list. The three men's first job was robbing a train depot in Nowata, Indian Territory. They escaped with seventeen hundred dollars.

Starr was caught soon after that robbery, and returned to Fort Smith jail. He pleaded "Not Guilty" at his arraignment, and was released on two thousand dollars bond. He returned to Indian Territory, with no intention of returning to Fort Smith for trial.

An arrest warrant was issued by U.S. Commissioner Stephen Wheeler for Starr's arrest on the prior horse stealing charge when Starr failed to appear in court. The warrant was given to Henry C. Dickey and Floyd Wilson to serve on Starr if they could find him.

Dickey and Wilson picked up Starr's trail near Lenapah, Indian Territory. It was rumored the Starr Gang would meet at Arthur Dodge's "XU" ranch.

Dodge denied knowing Starr personally, but admitted to the deputies he had seen him ride by his place several times lately. The following day, when the lawmen returned to the Dodge ranch for dinner, Dodge informed the marshals he had just seen Henry ride by that day.

Wilson rushed to his horse, already saddled, and headed off in the direction Henry had gone. Dickey was further behind as he had to saddle his mount.

Marshal Wilson found Henry in an opening on Wolf Creek. Wilson dropped from his saddle with a rifle in his hands. Facing Henry, who also held a rifle. Wilson ordered the outlaw to surrender, firing the rifle in the air as a warning.

Starr returned the gunfire and Wilson was hit and fell to the ground. Wilson's rifle jammed, and even though injured, he reached for his pistol. Starr fired two more shots and Wilson sank to the ground. Starr then advanced on the victim and fired another round into the lawman's heart.

Henry eluded the law until later that year, when he was caught in Colorado and extradited back to Fort Smith, Arkansas, where he would stand trial for Deputy Floyd Wilson's murder. Henry pleaded guilty to manslaughter and was sentenced to fifteen years in the penitentiary at Columbus, Ohio.

While in prison. Starr was able to help officials quell a riot. Crawford Goldsby, alias "Cherokee Bill", attempted a jailbreak. Goldsby had already killed one guard and barricaded himself in a cell.

Henry told officials he would go into Goldsby's cell and disarm him if they would not shoot Cherokee Bill. Cherokee Bill was an old acquaintance of Starr's, going back to their days with the Bill Cook Gang. The guards made the promise.

Once in the cell, Starr convinced his friend that he had no chance of escape. Cherokee Bill gave up his revolver and Starr turned it over to the guards.

Soon after his release from prison, with different partners, Starr participated in some minor robberies, none yielding more than four hundred dollars. The robberies heightened his interest in crime even though they failed to make him a rich man.

Starr wanted to pull a big job that would enhance his wealth and his notoriety. He settled on the Caney Bank, in Caney, Kansas. Frank Cheney, a farmer that had helped Starr rob a train depot and two general stores, joined him for this caper, too.

The two rode into Caney and entered the Caney National Bank. Cheney entered the vault carrying an old two-bushel sack.

He said, "I've kept this sack on my farm for seven years for this very purpose." He emerged from the vault with the sack almost filled with currency.

The bandits locked the bank's customers and employees in a back room and left the bank. At lest twenty five men were within calling distance of the bank, yet not a person knew what was going on inside until the robbers were on their horses and riding out of town.

They were ninety miles from Caney by dawn the next day. When they counted their loot, they learned they had taken forty nine hundred dollars from the bank, considerably less than they had expected. The bank's cashier, F.S. Hollingsworth, had managed to hide a stack of large denomination bills behind some ledger books, saving the bank sixteen thousand dollars.

Compared to his contemporaries in the outlaw world, Starr was well educated, although he had left school when he was only eleven years old.

Two other things distinguished Starr from bandits such as Jesse James, Bill Doolin, or Cherokee Bill. He was not a wanton killer. During his thirty-year outlaw career, Starr killed only one man, which he claimed was self-defense. Unfortunately, that man was a deputy Floyd Wilson.

Neither did he participate in drinking and carousing, even while those around him were getting drunk. He was determined to keep a clear head. When Milo Creekmore, Starr's partner in a successful robbery at Sequoyah, bought some whiskey to celebrate, Starr ended the partnership.

While heading west on a train, Starr was captured in Colorado Springs by four policemen and returned to Fort Smith for trial. He was found guilty of manslaughter and seven counts of robbery. He was transported to the federal prison at Columbus, Ohio, on January 15, 1898.

Starr managed to avoid hard labor by being a model prisoner at Columbus. His natural intelligence and obvious charm allowed him to gain the confidence of guards and prison officials.

In 1901, his mother visited Washington, D.C. and was allowed to speak to President Theodore Roosevelt. After hearing her story, Roosevelt wired Henry Starr and asked if he could behave if given a pardon? He quickly assured the president that he could.

He returned to Tulsa, worked in his mother's restaurant, married and had an only child, who he named, Theodore Roosevelt Starr.

Officials in Arkansas were not happy about Starr's release. They immediately sought his extradition for the robbery of the Bentonville Bank. To beat the extradition, Starr hit the road. He again hooked up with Kid Wilson, and they robbed the State Bank in Tyro, Kansas.

Starr then went into hiding in New Mexico. He made the mistake of writing a so-called friend back in Tulsa. That friend betrayed Starr to law officials. He stood trial for a robbery in Amity, Colorado and was imprisoned at Canon City, Colorado.

He was released after serving a short term and on the condition that he not leave the state of Colorado. He immediately returned to Oklahoma.

Between September 8, 1914 and January 13, 1915, Starr was accused of robbing fourteen different banks, all during the daylight. Starr denied that he had done the robberies.

Starr's next plan was to duplicate an attempt tried by the Dalton Gang. That was to rob two banks at the same time. He and his gang targeted the First National Bank and the Stroud National Bank in Oklahoma Territory.

While the gang escaped with some loot, Starr was shot, the victim of a young boy's "hog rifle." After he recovered from his wound, he was taken to the state penitentiary at McAlester.

Here, he convinced officials of his sincerity by speaking of the foolishness of a life of crime. He told a reporter for the Oklahoma World:

"I'm forty-five years old now, and seventeen of my forty-five years have been spent inside. Isn't that enough to tell any young boy that there's nothing to the kind of life I have led?" He was paroled again in the spring of 1919, his third and last early release.

He stayed straight for two years, even starring in a movie about the Stroud, Oklahoma bank robbery. The film was a success, but for some reason, Starr did not receive any money. He again turned to bank robbery.

He chose People's National Bank in Harrison, Arkansas. As Starr stepped into the vault, an employee of the bank seized a Winchester rifle kept in the vault for just such a purpose. He fired on Starr at point-blank range.

Four days later, Henry Starr died on February 22, 1921. While he was considered one of the most successful bandits in Western history, Starr, like most outlaws ended a failure.

Chapter 22

Jelly Bryce

'The FBI's Legendary Sharpshooter

D. A. "Jelly" Bryce could draw and fire a .357 Magnum in two-fifths of a second, faster than the human eye can follow. Writer K.B. Chaffin details the career of Jelly Bryce on Oklahombres Internet site.

Bryce could drop a silver dollar from shoulder height with his right hand, and then, with the same hand, draw and shoot the coin before it reached his waist.

Even as a child, Bryce was recognized as something of a prodigy with firearms. He was especially encouraged in his study of firearms by a doting grandfather who provided him with shotgun shells.

Jelly Bryce

Bryce is said to have saved more than one hundred dollars as a youngster by shining shoes, all of which he invested in ammunition. In those days, one hundred dollars would have purchased quite a load of ammunition.

When Bryce graduated from high school, he was driving to enroll in the University of Oklahoma. Along the way, he heard of a pistol contest. The winner would receive one hundred dollars in gold as first prize. This really caught his attention.

The contest was in Shawnee, Oklahoma, held as part of the annual Oklahoma Sheriff's and Peace Officers convention. When Bryce arrived at the firing range, he got out of his car and approached Clarence Hurt, then Night Chief of Police and a member of the Oklahoma City pistol team.

"This contest open to anybody?" he asked Hurt.

"You think you can shoot, huh?" Hurt asked.

"I think I can, yes," Bryce replied.

Hurt was unsure, a young kid in white slacks and a sweater approaching him out of the blue. Besides that, he was shooting an old smoothbore .38 that was nearly an antique.

The Oklahoma City pistol team did need some help if they were going to win, and Hurt knew that was impossible with the team they had.

The two walked behind a hill so Hurt could see what the youngster could do.

"What do you want me to shoot," Bryce asked.

The officer took out an old envelope and stuck in the cleft of a tree trunk and walked off the regulation distance. "Shoot that", he told the Youngster.

"Can I draw and shoot," Bryce asked. "I'm better if I draw first than just standing still."

"Up to you," replied Hurt.

Bryce drew and put six fast shots into an area the size of a silver dollar.

Speechless, Hurt said, "You are now a member of the Oklahoma City Police Department.

Bryce won the hundred dollars, and his team won the contest. He also launched into a new career.

It did not take long for Bryce to develop a reputation with the Oklahoma Police Department. He was barely indoctrinated when he had to call on his speed with a firearm.

As the story goes, Bryce, in plain clothes, was leaving a restaurant in downtown Oklahoma City at high noon. He saw a man sitting in a nearby car, furtively looking around and very nervous.

Bryce walked over to the driver's side of the car and opened the door. The man inside looked up, startled. He had some tools and it appeared he was trying to start the car without a key.

"What are you doing," Bryce asked.

"Who are you?" the man snarled.

"A police officer."

Without another word, the man drew a pistol from under his coat. Before he could fire, Bryce drew and killed him.

The worst wasn't over. Onlookers called the police to report the killing. Bryce hadn't been issued a badge yet. When police arrived, the police captain didn't know him. He was arrested for murder and taken to jail.

Fortunately, Clarence Hurt, who had hired him, showed up that night and turned him loose.

The comedy of errors continues. Bryce's father heard about the murder on the news before Bryce was released. He arrived in Oklahoma City with a lawyer. While relieved that no charges were being filed, he urged his son to return home to small town life.

"I've never disobeyed you before this," he told his father, "but this is what I want to do. I want to be a policeman."

Being a police officer in the 1920s and 1930s was anything but peaceful. Consider, for instance, that in 1932, there were 59 bank robberies in Oklahoma, but only 30 robbed in 1933. The Oklahoma City Times joked that the economy was so bad even bank robbery was in a slump.

During this time period, the media was glamorizing bank robbers and criminals. It was open season on police officers.

One night in 1927, Bryce was alone on night patrol. He saw two men in an alley trying to jimmy the back door of a furniture store. He swerved his patrol car into the mouth of the alley, and stopped with his headlights trained on the pair. As he jumped from the car, the men spun and both fired at the same time.

Bryce killed them both instantly with just two shots.

Oklahoma City detectives learned that Outlaw Harvey Pugh, once a companion of Clyde Barrow, was holed up at the Wren Hotel. Pugh was wanted for the murder of a police officer in McPherson, Kansas.

Bryce and two other detectives were dispatched to arrest Pugh and question the two other men holed up with him.

When they entered the seedy hotel, they told the elderly woman at the front desk they wanted to see the owner, 28-year-old Mrs. Merle Bolen. The woman led them up the dark stairway and down a dingy hallway.

The old lady tapped on the door and opened it. But before the detectives could enter she tried to pull the door closed. "I told you we're police officers," growled Bryce, sticking his foot in the door.

He shoved the door open to see Mrs. Bolen, in skimpy pajamas, lying on the bed with J. Ray O'Donnell, one of the gangsters the officers wanted to question. O'Donnell was aiming two automatic pistols at Bryce.

Bryce's own .38 was still holstered under his coat. In a single blur, Bryce drew and killed O'Donnell before he could pull the trigger. The officers arrested both women and Tom Watson. When Harvey Pugh returned to pick up his automobile, they nailed him too.

The detective reportedly got his nickname "Jelly" for the dapper way he dressed. Once, when he was chasing a gangster, he followed the crook into a theater. He asked the manager to turn up the theater lights.

The outlaw had crawled up a carpeted stairway, mortally wounded and barely conscious. The dying crook looked up at Bryce and said, "I can't believe I was killed by a jelly bean like you." When the remark was repeated in the newspapers, he quickly became known as "Jelly", but it was nickname he grew to like.

It was Bryce who perfected the stance adopted by law enforcement agencies around the country. In his stance, he would shift his body slightly forward so that if he were hit, he would fall forward and be able to keep firing.

He left the Oklahoma City Police Department in 1934 to go with the FBI. He is known as one of those that brought down the Barker Gang.

Bryce was able to do tricks with firearms that few others could duplicate. This made him popular to perform demonstrations for the FBI.

One of his more unusual stunts was with a .22 Caliber rifle. He would have someone toss a Mexican peso in the air and he would shoot it. But first he announced that he would put the bullet close to the edge so that it would make a good watch fob. Witnesses say he never missed.

Bryce was said to not only be a superb shot, but had almost supernatural eyesight. He once claimed he could actually follow the trajectory of a bullet as it left the gun and sped toward a target.

He reportedly killed at least nineteen criminals during his career.

When asked if he was interested in bringing any of them back alive, he replied, "I'm more interested in bringing me back alive."

At the time he was in charge of the El Paso office, he made a trip to Roswell, New Mexico. He saw what he thought was the most beautiful girl he had ever seen crossing the street.

Bryce went up to her, introduced himself, and said, "I just thought you'd want to know, I'm going to marry you."

He did. Her name was Shirley Bloodworth. Unfortunately, she died as the result of a car wreck after he retired. Her death devastated Bryce.

Bryce died in his hotel room from a heart attack while attending a reunion of retired police officers.

Chapter 23

John Dillinger

The entire country was in a depression. Banks were closing and foreclosing right and left, taking the life savings of millions.

It is little wonder that the populace cheered when bank robbers such as John Dillinger, Harry Pierpont, Baby Face Nelson and the rest of the Dillinger Gang would wipe out a bank. It was an especially happy day when the robbers destroyed the bank's mortgage records in the process.

John Dillinger

J. Edgar Hoover, head of the FBI wasn't as entertained by the Dillinger Gang's activities as the citizenry was when these Midwestern crime sprees took place. Hoover saw Dillinger and his gang as a threat to the national morals. Dillinger was Public Enemy No. 1, and lived up to the title bestowed on him by Hoover.

Harry Pierpont, a Dillinger accomplice, explained himself this way: "I stole from the bankers who stole from the people." This reasoning did not hold water with Mr. Hoover.

Hoover quickly had new crime laws enacted that made bank robbery, transportation of stolen goods or flight of a felon over state lines to avoid prosecution a national crime. The laws brought these criminals under the jurisdiction of the FBI.

Dillinger's career in crime started with a botched robbery attempt of a grocer in his hometown of Mooresville, Indiana. He had just turned 21 three months earlier. He was sent to reformatory in Pendleton, Indiana.

He requested and received a transfer to Indiana State Prison in Michigan City, Indiana, where Harry Pierpont and Homer Van Meter were jailed. They would become a part of John Dillinger's gang.

Dillinger was a brutal thief and cold-blooded murderer. From September 1933, until July 1934, he and his gang terrorized the Midwest, killing ten men and wounding seven others. They robbed banks and police arsenals. The gang staged three jailbreaks, killing a sheriff during one and wounding two guards in another.

Committing a string of bank robberies and other crimes across country, Dillinger became a national news item. While he was incarcerated in Pima County jail, in Arizona, newspapermen and photographers poured in from everywhere.

Dillinger and his gang gave interviews, while behind the scenes there was a lot of legal wrangling over which state would win extradition.

He was eventually extradited to Indiana to stand trial for killing patrolman William O'Malley during the robbery of the First National Bank in East Chicago, Indiana.

On January 30, 1934, Dillinger, with a contingent of guards, arrived at Chicago Municipal Airport. He was greeted by an even larger contingent of police, in addition to the FBI's so-called "Dillinger Squad".

Dillinger was going to the supposedly "escape proof" Crown Point County Jail in Indiana. Rumors persisted that he would pull an escape. Authorities seemed unconcerned because of the heavy guard at the jail.

One morning, when an elderly jail attendant unlocked the door to the cellblock so trusties could to the morning cleanup, John Dillinger stuck what appeared to be a gun in the jail attendant's stomach and ordered him into the cell.

Dillinger then ordered the attendant to call Deputy Sheriff Ernest Blunk and Warden Lou Baker. These men he placed in the cell with the jail attendant.

With machine guns taken from the warden's office, Dillinger captured a dozen guards, which he also herded into cells.

He then took a couple of hostages with him in the sheriff's car and drove madly across the Illinois state line where the hostages were released.

Red-faced officials later learned the weapon that allowed Dillinger to pull off his escape was only crudely carved piece of dark wood.

Heading straight for Chicago, Dillinger recruited a new gang. Within days after the escape from Crown Point, they robbed the Security National Bank and Trust in Sioux Falls, South Dakota.

Dillinger escaped the many traps the FBI set for him. He was in need of a place where he and his gang could hide out. They selected "Little Bohemia", a summer resort in northern Wisconsin. Since it was still off-season, the lodge had rooms.

But when Emil Wanatka and his wife Nan, who had built the lodge, found out who their customers were they were terrified.

They got word to the FBI about the Dillinger Gang's whereabouts, but the FBI's plan to capture them went awry for a variety of reasons. Hoover had promised the newspapers something special, but the fiasco left him with egg on his face.

Dillinger stayed just ahead of police and FBI agents for some time. In Washington, FBI Director Hoover assigned Special Agent Samuel A. Cowley to head the FBI's investigative efforts against Dillinger. He joined with Melvin Purvis, in the FBI's Chicago office to plan their strategy and track down all tips and rumors.

A break in the case came when a madam in a Gary, Indiana brothel called police with information. She called herself Anna Sage, however, her real name was Ana Cumpanas. She had entered the United States from Rumania, but because of her profession was considered an undesirable alien.

Anna was willing to sell information about Dillinger for a cash reward plus help in preventing her deportation. Agent's Cowley and Purvis were cautious. They promised her the reward if her information led to Dillinger's capture, but could not promise safety from deportation. They would call attention to her cooperation with the Department of Labor, however.

Anna told the agents that she, Polly Hamilton, and Dillinger would be going to the movies the following evening. She said she would be wearing a red dress.

At 10:30 p.m., Dillinger, with his two female companions on either side, walked out of the theater and turned to his left. FBI Agent Purvis was hiding in a doorway. As Dillinger walked by, he lit a cigar as a signal to other FBI agents.

Five shots were fired from the guns of three FBI agents. Three of the shots hit Dillinger and he fell face down on the pavement. He was pronounced dead twenty minutes later in the Alexian Brothers Hospital. He was 31 years old.

Eventually, twenty-seven people were convicted in federal courts on charges of harboring, aiding and abetting John Dillinger and his cronies during their reign of terror.

Chapter 24

Charles 'Pretty Boy' Floyd

He was often called "The People's Bandit" because of his habit of burning mortgages held by banks during his robberies, which essentially gave folks free homes and farms.

His family was dirt poor. His father spent most of his time trying to stay one step ahead of foreclosure. This may be one of the reason's Floyd liked to burn bank mortgages.

In an effort to keep the family fed, Floyd's father got involved in bootlegging.

While only seventeen-years- old, he married sixteen-

Charles 'Pretty Boy' Floyd

year- old Ruby Hargrove. Money was scarce for Floyd, so he left home to look for harvest work. He was willing to work, but there was no work. He spent many nights in hobo camps. Eventually, he quit looking for work and bought his first gun.

At the age of eighteen, he pulled his first crime. He held up a post office for $350 in pennies. He was arrested on suspicion of the crime, but his father gave him an alibi.

He took a train to St. Louis and robbed a Kroger store of about sixteen thousand dollars. Floyd and his wife spent the money on expensive clothes and big meals and in a few weeks, were broke again.

Floyd easily aroused police suspicions with his new clothes and a new Ford automobile. Police found some of the money still in its wrapper. He was sentenced to five years in the Jefferson City Penitentiary.

While he was still in prison, his wife gave birth to their son, Jack Dempsey Floyd, and divorced him.

When he visited his parent's farm while on parole, he discovered his father had been shot to death in a family feud with J. Mills. Mills was acquitted of the crime. Floyd took his father's rifle into the hills. J. Mills was never seen again.

Floyd then became a hired gun for bootleggers along the Ohio River. He then headed west and found employment in "Tom's Town", now Kansas City. It was a town run by Tom Pendegast where hired guns, murderers and successful gangsters hung out.

He learned to use a machine gun and acquired the name "Pretty Boy". A brothel madam, Beulah Baird Ash, gave the name to him and he hated it. The name stuck.

During the next twelve years, Floyd robbed as many as thirty banks and killed ten men. During his crime sprees in Oklahoma the bank insurance rates doubled.

Floyd was accused of taking part in the Kansas City Massacre at the Union Station. Some say this was strictly an FBI cover-up and that Floyd played no part in that event. The FBI, however, maintained that one FBI agent identified Floyd as he sped away from the scene.

Another story the FBI put out was that Floyd tried to free Frank Nash while he was being taken to prison, although Floyd did not even know Frank Nash personally. The FBI succeeded in pinning it on Floyd but never had any proof of his involvement.

The FBI intensified its hunt for both "Pretty Boy" Floyd and for Adam Richetti, who was identified as taking part in the Kansas City Massacre.

While traveling near Wellsville, Ohio, with Richetti and Beulah and Rose Baird, Floyd skidded their automobile into a telephone pole. He and Richetti removed their guns from the car and stayed on the outskirts of town, while Beulah and Rose took the vehicle in to have repairs made.

Curious neighbors reported to the Wellsville, Ohio police that two suspicious-looking men were seen on the outskirts of town. When the police chief found them resting in a wooded tract, a gun battle ensued.

Richetti was captured, but Floyd escaped. But the police chief believed that Floyd might have been wounded in the gunplay.

Lawmen widened their search. Officers noticed an automobile move from behind a corncrib on a farm. When they stopped their cars, the vehicle pulled back behind the corncrib.

A man whom the officers recognized as Floyd jumped from the car with a .45 caliber pistol in his right hand. Floyd surrendered without shooting, however, saying, "I'm done for; you've hit me twice."

Floyd died about fifteen minutes later.

In one interview, Floyd told Vivian Brown, a reporter, "I never shot at a fellow in my life unless I was forced into it by some trap being thrown to catch me and then it was that or else."

The minute John Dillinger was killed, Floyd jumped to number one on the FBI's "Public Enemy Number One list.

Chapter 25

Luke Short

Historians depict Luke Short as somewhat of a dandy. He was known to be good friends with both Bat Masterson and Wyatt Earp.

His great-nephew Wayne Short, author of "Luke Short: A Biography", writes one episode that portrays Luke.

"Luke Short was grabbed from behind and pulled off the boardwalk in front of the Oriental Saloon. He whirled and saw Charlie Storms beginning to draw. Luke pulled his short-barreled Colt and fired. The .45 caliber bullet slammed into Charlie Storms' heart.

Luke Short

He stood there a moment looking down at Storms, then turned to his companion Bat Masterson. "You sure as hell pick some of the damnedest people for friends, Bat!"

Luke hunted buffalo for their hides during the years 1874-75. He was once arrested for trading whiskey to Indians for buffalo robes. He escaped the army escort taking him to Omaha for trial on this charge.

His biography notes that he made his way to Denver, and never again worked except as a high rolling professional gambler.

Luke was the son of a sharecropper, born in 1854. He always remained thin as a rail. His stature attracted the notice of Judge Stordon, a horseman from Nashville. Stordon took Luke under his wing and taught him jockeying.

When Stordon thought his young protégé was ready, they headed for Hot Springs, Arkansas. Short won several races, endearing him to the ladies. He became so adept at blackjack and poker that he won the purses of riders and grooms in jockey rooms. Stordon was impressed with Short's gambling prowess.

The two then posed as indolent transients. They pooled their money and visited all the gambling parlors in St. Louis, New Orleans and San Francisco.

When Stordon died of a heart attack, Short struck out on his own, carrying a leather gripsack filled with double eagles and a hidden pistol to protect himself and his investment.

He started wearing fancy attire, and among the miners he fleeced, became known as "the gentleman gambler."

Eventually, bad luck overtook him, and he ended up broke. He then returned to the cow towns, working as a bartender and part-time house gambler.

For ten years, Dodge City, Kansas was said to thrive on whiskey. City politics revolved around whiskey and

Dodge became known as the "Wickedest Little City in America".

Colonel Richard I. Dodge assumed command of Fort Dodge in 1872 and stopped the sale of alcohol at the fort. This edict affected not only the soldiers, but also the buffalo hunters and traders in western Kansas.

At the same time, the Atchison, Topeka & Santa Fe Railroad was laying track toward Fort Dodge, bringing hundreds of workers, most of whom wanted whiskey.

George Kennedy, a twenty-four-year-old Canadian, seized on what he thought was a masterful profit-making idea. He brought a wagonload of whiskey back from eastern Kansas to Fort Dodge. He set up five miles outside of Fort Dodge and opened for business, charging twenty-five cents a drink and became a wealthy man.

Luke Short bought the Long Branch Saloon in Dodge City. He soon became the target of an organized group called the Commercial Detective Agency. This was, in reality, a front for extorting money from saloons and gambling casinos. The chief collector was "Longhaired" Jim Courtright, considered one of the fastest draws in Texas.

His cross draw gave him the reputation of being equal to, if not superior, to the likes of Wild Bill Hickok, Johnny Ringo, and Wes Hardin. Most saloon owners generally paid up rather than go against Courtright.

One evening, Courtright strolled into Luke Short's saloon to collect the extortion money.

"Go to Hell!" Luke told him

"I'll be back," Courtright snarled, "and you'd better pay up!"

While Short's friends urged him to comply with Courtright's demands, Luke remained adamant.

When Courtright returned the next evening, Short was running the roulette wheel. Courtright asked him for the money.

"I have no intention of paying, is that plain enough," Short told him.

Longhaired Jim went for his gun, but Short beat him to the draw. He fired a split second before Courtright, severing the extortionist's thumb on his gun hand. When Courtright attempted to toss his gun to his other hand, Luke fired again. The bullet caught Courtright squarely between the eyes.

W.H. Harris, a candidate for mayor, was a partner in Luke's saloon. The opposition candidate for mayor backed Luke's saloon competition.

When the election was held, Harris lost and the new mayor passed ordinances to suppress brothels and vagrants. Two days later, three women employed as singers in Luke's Long Branch Saloon were arrested. No similar arrests were made at competing saloons, however.

Saloonkeepers, including Luke Short, who were not favored by the new mayor were arrested under the city's new anti-gambling laws and told to get on the next train that was leaving town. Some 150 citizens were put on watch to make sure they did not come back.

Luke settled in Kansas City, and was kept informed of the situation in Dodge City, where the tension continued to escalate. Bat Masterson came to Kansas City to help his friend Luke Short.

Masterson was ex-sheriff of Ford County and had previously crossed with the same men now faced by Luke Short. A short time later, more of Luke's friends arrived, including Wyatt Earp, Joe Lowe, known as "Rowdy Joe", Shotgun Collins, and Doc Holliday.

The news that these famous gunslingers were joining Luke Short in his fight against Dodge City's mayor did cause a furor. The matter was eventually settled when the city allowed Short to pay a one-thousand-dollar-fine and reopen his business.

Gambling was again legalized and ornate screen doors were put on the front of the establishments to bar the view of passersby.

Luke sold the Long Branch in 1884. With the money from the sale, he opened up the White Elephant saloon in Fort Worth, Texas. The establishment had a luxurious billiard room. The money rolled in.

During his early days, Luke was referred to as a "white Indian". He is said to have been an Indian in every respect except color. He was a little fellow, only about five feet, six inches in height, and weighing perhaps one hundred forty pounds soaking wet.

His head was somewhat larger than the rest of his body. It required a seven-and-one-eighth-inch hat to fit his well-shaped round head.

Luke Short had received none of the advantages in school. He could barely write his name legibly. After Luke left home at thirteen years of age for cutting up a school bully, he worked as a thirty-dollar-a-month cowboy, driving cattle from Texas to the Kansas rail towns.

Frank Dowler, and old-time sheriff of Palmdale, California, knew well Luke Short's history.

"Seldom did anyone make a laughing remark about his height, or the fact the name Short might refer to his shortness."

Short was sometimes referred to as "Dapper Luke". He wore a silk, stovepipe hat, a fancy braided shirt with ruffles, and a diamond stickpin in his tie.

Some referred to Luke Short as the "Undertaker's Friend," because he "shot 'em where it didn't show."

In August 1893, Luke, his wife, and his brother, Young, went to Geuda Springs in Sumner County to bathe in the health-restoring waters. Luke had dropsy. In less than a month, he died. His remains were buried in Oakwood Cemetery in Fort Worth.

Chapter 26

Tom Horn

Tom Horn may best known as the man who tracked down and talked Indian Chief Geronimo into surrendering.

But he perhaps should be known also as a man who wove a rope that was later used to hang him.

Horn, born in Memphis, Missouri in 1860, worked both sides of the law during his career. After a savage beating by his father when he was fourteen, Horn ran away from home. He became a scout for the army at age sixteen.

His abilities as an army scout were well recognized. He worked for Al Sieber who took

Tom Horn

young Tom under his wing and turned him into a number one scout. Horn and Sieber met with Pedro, Chief of the friendly Apaches, who took the young scout into his tribe like it was his own.

179

Tom lived like and was an Apache. He learned to speak both Apache and Spanish like a native. During his time with the Apaches the Army was paying him as an interpreter. He thoroughly loved his job.

Horn lost his job when the government started the first military Indian Agency in 1877. This meant that no white man could live on a reservation.

For a while, Horn worked as a prospector, searching for silver. Along with Sieber, he staked a claim, but it failed to produce much. They sold it for $2,800.

Tom and Sieber then started hunting game for a mining camp. They would get two dollars and fifty cents for every deer they brought in. One day, a detachment of soldiers rode up on Tom and Sieber while they were hunting and handed them a letter from General Wilcox.

The letter informed them that they were again under pay and for them to report to Fort Whipple at once. Tom was reinstated as an interpreter.

Horn replaced Sieber as chief of scouts in 1886. His job: go get Geronimo. As chief of scouts, he tracked Geronimo and his band to a hideout in the Sierra Gordo outside of Senora, Mexico. Alone, he rode into the Indian camp and negotiated Geronimo's surrender.

With Horn guiding, Geronimo and his tribe crossed the border, officially surrendering. This ended the last great Indian war in America.

He quit his post as chief of scouts, eventually going to work as a cowboy. He became so adept at roping he entered a rodeo at Globe, Arizona, in 1888 and won the world's championship in steer roping.

Horn next joined the Pinkerton Detective Agency in 1890, working out of the agency's Denver offices. His job involved chasing bank and train robbers throughout Colorado and Wyoming.

He was fearless and would stand up against any outlaw or gunman. On one occasion, Horn rode into the outlaw hideout known as "Hole-in-the-Wall" to capture Peg-Leg Watson (alias McCoy) who had recently robbed a mail train.

He tracked the thief to a high mountain cabin. As he approached, he called out, "Watson, I'm coming for you."

Watson stepped outside the cabin, holding a six-gun in each hand. He watched, open-mouthed as Horn walked resolutely across an open field toward him, his Winchester carried limply at his side.

Without firing a shot, Horn took Watson to jail. Horn became a legend for his daring.

As an agent for the Pinkertons, Tom had killed seventeen men. He didn't like hunting down men that were much like himself. He handed in his badge, saying, "I have no stomach for it anymore."

His next job belied his words. He went to work as a horse breaker for the Swan Land and Cattle Company. His real job, however, was to track down and kill rustlers and to harass settlers homesteading the range. He demanded and got six hundred dollars for each rustler he shot.

Horn was meticulous in his job. He would spend days tracking a rustler, learning the man's habits. Horn would then lay a careful ambush and, with a high-powered Buffalo gun, kill the rustler with a single well-aimed bullet.

Horn was no longer the righteous gunman who faced adversaries in a fair fight. He killed from hiding and he killed often. More than a dozen rustlers were found shot to death on the range.

He left a large rock under the head of each rustler he killed. This became his trademark. The residents of Wyoming learned to fear the gunman. Horn's last killing proved to be his undoing.

He was hunting down Kels P. Nickell, who had been marked for death by competing ranchers. Horn had only seen Nickell once and then only from a distance.

As Willie Nickell, the fourteen-year-old son of the rancher, drove his father's wagon out of the ranch yard, he wore his father's coat and hat. When he got off the wagon to open a gate, Horn fired.

The boy staggered, and then tried to get back into the wagon. Horn fired again, striking him in the back of the head, killing him.

Joe Lefors, considered the best lawman in the west, determined to bring Horn in, though the only evidence that Horn had done the killing was he was noted for his long-distance killings.

The deputy rode to Denver. Meeting with Horn, who did not know Lefors, the lawman was able to get Tom drunk in a saloon. Deputies, with a crude listening device, were in a back room.

Lefors got Tom to talking about the Nickell killing. He described it in such detail that he was, in fact, confessing. Lefors arrested and returned Horn to Cheyenne.

Horn spent his last months writing his memoirs and weaving the rope that would be used to hang him. He was hanged November 20, 1903.

Chapter 27

Edward O. Kelly

The man that killed Jesse James is generally well known. But how many people know who killed the man that killed Jesse James?

As the reader probably knows, Robert Ford was the man that shot Jesse in the back in order to collect the big reward on his head. Ford has come down in both song and story, but not necessarily as a hero. Some say he was a coward.

When Robert Ford left Missouri, pretty much in disgrace for killing the famous outlaw Jesse James, he went to New Mexico. He first settled in Las Vegas, New Mexico, and then moved to Walsenburg, Colorado.

He opened a saloon and gambling hall. It was here, according to writer Jim Cloud that Ford became thought of as a desperado. He was involved in many shooting scrapes, in most of which he was the aggressor.

He boasted often about his feat in killing Jesse James, and ridding the country of the most famous outlaw the west had ever known.

Ford was especially mean when he was drinking, which became more and more frequent. When he was drunk, he liked to shoot out the lights in saloons and other public places.

Ford soon decided to pack his gambling apparatus and move to Creede, Colorado, the site of a big silver rush. One evening, Ford and a drinking companion went into the street and began shooting out lights and destroying property.

This didn't sit well with Creede residents. The next day, Ford was ordered out of town by four o'clock in the afternoon or face the penalty of forfeiting his life. To escape the vigilante action, Ford left for Pueblo by train.

It was in Pueblo where Ed Kelly met Bob Ford by accident. By mutual agreement, the two men shared a room.

Ford was attempting to negotiate his return to Creede. He was writing letters to businessmen and town leaders to get them to relent. He even wrote an apology to the editor of the Creede newspaper. His letters all went unanswered.

One morning, when Ford awoke, he saw that Ed Kelly had left. Depending on which account one accepts, Ford claimed that he was missing either a diamond ring or a diamond scarf pin. There are some reports the two men had a quarrel over a woman.

Kelly resented Ford's accusation that he was the one that stole the diamond jewelry. Ford then got word that he could return to Creede, the silver city, and reopen his gambling emporium.

Ed Kelly, who was now marshal for Bachelor City, went to Creede one day and wandered into Bob Ford's saloon. When Ford saw him, he started a racket, and took a knife and gun away from Kelly. He then beat Kelly over the head with a pistol.

He threatened to shoot Marshal Ed Kelly if he ever set foot in his saloon again. The hate between the two men continued to grow as Kelly headed back for Bachelor City.

On Sunday, June 5, 1892, a fire burned down most of the town of Creede, including Bob Ford's establishment.

Bob secured property for a tent building and reopened his dancehall and gambling business.

One day after Ford reopened his business, Ed Kelly entered with a shotgun. He walked toward Kelly, whose back was toward him. Ed called, "Hello Bob." As Ford turned, Kelly fired both barrels. Bob Ford fell to the floor, dead, much the scenario that happened when Ford shot Jesse James in the back.

Kelly retreated from the building and surrendered to Deputy Sheriff Dick Plunkett. A jury ordered that Kelly be held over for trial as he had committed the murder with felonious intent.

Deputy Sheriff Gardiner took charge of Kelly, placing him in a vacant building, which guarded against a possible lynching. Ed Kelly was taken to Lake City, Colorado for trial.

When asked by the judge Ed pleaded "Not Guilty!" A jury was empanelled for that afternoon. The jury found Kelly guilty of murder in the second degree. Kelly appeared before the judge four days later for sentencing. He was given a life term in the penitentiary at hard labor.

Kelly was imprisoned on July 13, 1892. He won a parole and was discharged October 3, 1902. Reports say he returned to Pueblo, and then next appeared in Oklahoma City.

Police in Oklahoma City placed him under surveillance. He was believed to be one of a gang suspected of burglaries in Oklahoma City.

In December 1903, Policeman Joe Burnett arrested Kelly as a suspicious character. Kelly was offended, and soon after, he let it be known he was looking for a certain man, namely Joe Burnett. The two met while the policeman was walking his beat. Kelly struck at the policemen and a fight ensued.

When Burnett finally got a gun hand free with the help of a railroad baggage man, he shot Ed Kelly.

Ed Kelly, age forty-six, was interned at Fairlawn Cemetery in north Oklahoma City. The county provided the casket at a cost of twelve dollars and fifty cents.

187

188

189

191

About the Author

Alton Pryor has been a writer for magazines, newspapers, and wire services for more than 35 years. He worked for United Press International in their Sacramento Bureau, handling both printed press as well as radio news.

He then journeyed to Salinas, where he worked for the Salinas Californian daily newspaper for five years.

In 1963, he joined California Farmer magazine where he worked as a field editor for 27 years. When that magazine was sold, the new owners forced him into retirement, which did not suit him at all.

He then turned to writing books. Alton Pryor is the author of four books, "Little Known Tales in California History", "Classic Tales in California History", "Those Wild and Lusty Gold Camps" and "Jonathan's Red Apple Tree", and "Outlaws and Gunslingers.

He is a graduate of California State Polytechnic University, San Luis Obispo, where he earned a Bachelor of Science degree in journalism.

Order Form

Stagecoach Publishing
5360 Campcreek Loop
Roseville, Ca. 95747-8009
(916) 771-8166
Fax: (916) 771-8166

Please send

____ copies	"Little Known Tales in California History"	$9.95
____ copies	"Classic Tales in California History"	9.95
____ copies	"Jonathan's Red Apple Tree"	4.95
____ copies	"Those Wild and Lusty Gold Camps"	6.95
____ copies	"Outlaws and Gunslingers"	9.95

Name:_____

Address:_____

City:_____ State:_____ Zip:_____

Telephone: (___)_____

Shipping and handling: $3.00 for first book, and $1.00 each additional book.

Signature_____